REVISED EDITION

PRACTISE
WRITING

Mary Stephens

Contents

Writing for the Cambridge First Certificate examination

Most people feel nervous about writing for examinations but if you read widely and practise the steps outlined in this book you should have no worries on examination day! Here are the answers to questions commonly asked by examination candidates.

What kind of tasks will I have to do in the First Certificate (Paper 2)?

You will have to carry out two tasks.

Part One is compulsory. You will see 1–3 short texts and sometimes some pictures. Using the information you get from these and from the rubric (instructions) you must write a letter of 120–180 words.

Part Two. You choose *one* task (120–180 words) from a choice of four. This could be one of the following: a friendly or formal letter, an article, a report (maybe on a place you have visited – a country, city, or building), a job application, an opinion, a narrative or a description. You can also choose to write about a background text/set book. In this case you may be asked to write an article, a letter or a report or describe a book cover in relation to the text (also 120–180 words).

You will have 1 hour 30 minutes for the whole exam.

What are the most important things to consider before I actually start to write?

Writing is a form of communication, just as much as speaking. You do not speak to your bank manager or doctor in the same way you speak to the people you love! It is just the same when you write. You will need to think about who is going to read your piece of writing and what impression you want to make. Look at the extracts below and on page 4. In each case, say who you think the text was written for. What is it about the appearance and the language of the text which helps you to decide?

16 O'Donnell Street
Castlebar
County Mayo
Ireland

16 June, 199-

Dear Sue,
    It seems hard to believe that I've been here in Irelan
for a whole week now! I promised to write and tell you hou
I was getting on – so here goes!
    When I first got here, I just couldn't get used to the
slow pace of life! Now, though, I'm learning to take things
easy – and I'm beginning to feel really really at home. My first
impression of the Irish is that they are really, really friendly
and helpful – and they certainly know how to enjoy life!
The countryside round about is marvellous – and very green
because it rains a lot! I've already done some fishing and
sailing and have made friends with some of the young
people in the village. We spend most evenings in the local
bar which has a real peat fire and great music – and
    I've managed to rent a little cottage here in Castlebar

To: Ms K Lett
From: Anna Santini
Subject: Brightsea Beach Language School

We visited Brightsea Beach at the end of our trip to England (August 4-12,) and were very impressed by the school and by the environment.

The School: *This* is made up of four separate houses, linked by beautiful gardens. Although classrooms are quite small, they are light and airy. There is a fully-equipped computer centre in the main building, and a well-stocked library.

Always ask yourself the following questions:

- *Who* am I writing to? Should I be friendly or formal?
- *Why* am I writing this – to explain, to persuade, to apologise, to inform, to amuse, to give facts?
- *What effect* do I want to have on the person who reads this?
- *What style* do I need to use to achieve this effect?
- Should the text be *formal* or *informal*?
- What sort of *layout* should I use?

Which skills are the examiners looking for?

To write a good text (and please the examiner) you should be able to:

- answer the question that is asked, not the one you think is being asked, or would prefer! Keep looking back to the question and checking you are keeping to the point.
- organise your ideas into paragraphs, with a key sentence in each paragraph. Make sure your paragraphs consist of a number of sentences (not just one) grouped round one central idea.
- link your paragraphs together.
- use a good range of grammatical structures and tenses.
- connect your sentences in a variety of ways. Do not just use *and* or *but*.
- begin with an interesting introduction which catches the reader's attention.
- use a range of vocabulary. Try to choose a good selection of adjectives and adverbs for descriptions.
- spell correctly.
- punctuate correctly.
- write an interesting ending. Do not just stop in mid air because time ran out!

How can I improve my writing?

Long before the examination try and write as much as you can. Writing gets easier the more you practise! Try keeping a diary, or get yourself a pen friend. Now is the time to develop your writing skills. Keep to the processes you meet in this book:

- **Make a plan** by brainstorming ideas on a scrap of paper. Sometimes you will find a linear plan most useful, at other times a spidergraph or just headings, may be better (see below). When you have finished, check through and eliminate any unimportant items. Number the remaining items in a logical order. Use this as a guide for paragraphing.

- **Write a first draft.**

- **Make any necessary changes.**
  Check that you have kept to the question.
  Add details if necessary, or eliminate irrelevant information.
  Check your paragraphs. Add linking words if necessary.
  Check if your first and final paragraphs need improving. If necessary, try out different versions on a separate piece of paper.
  Check grammar, spelling (concentrate on words you often get wrong) and punctuation

- **Write a second draft.**

- **Assess yourself!** Make sure your work is clearly set out and your handwriting is legible. Ask a friend to check spelling and punctuation with you.

- **Write a third draft if necessary.**

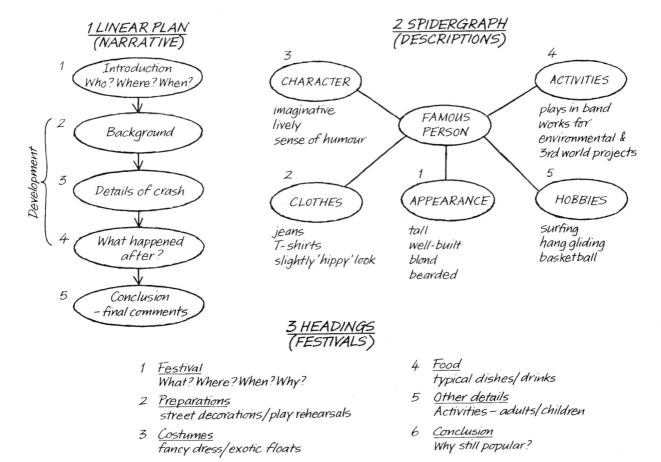

1 LINEAR PLAN (NARRATIVE)

1 Introduction — Who? Where? When?
2 Background
3 Details of crash
4 What happened after?
5 Conclusion – final comments

Development (2, 3, 4)

2 SPIDERGRAPH (DESCRIPTIONS)

FAMOUS PERSON

3 CHARACTER
imaginative
lively
sense of humour

4 ACTIVITIES
plays in band
works for environmental & 3rd world projects

2 CLOTHES
jeans
T-shirts
slightly 'hippy' look

1 APPEARANCE
tall
well-built
blond
bearded

5 HOBBIES
surfing
hang gliding
basketball

3 HEADINGS (FESTIVALS)

1 Festival
What? Where? When? Why?

2 Preparations
street decorations/play rehearsals

3 Costumes
fancy dress/exotic floats

4 Food
typical dishes/drinks

5 Other details
Activities – adults/children

6 Conclusion
Why still popular?

Will it be difficult to write to a time limit?

In the examination you will only have 45 minutes to answer each question. You will not have time for redrafting, so it is especially important to make a plan before you start writing. If you do not, you and your reader will probably end up being very confused!

Two or three months before the examination, set yourself a time limit for written work and try to keep to it. In that way, you will have a good idea how long to leave yourself for each part of the Writing Paper – and you will be used to writing under pressure when the great day comes!

I always make careless mistakes. How can I learn to correct them?

You may find it useful to keep a list of the kinds of words you commonly misspell, or a list of tenses you often misuse. When you finish writing a text, you can use this list to check for errors.

To help you learn to correct your own errors, your teacher may use a CORRECTION CODE like the one below. (If your teacher doesn't use a code, you can always work with a partner to find each other's mistakes using the same techniques.)

T = tense	**W O** = word order
G = grammar	**Adj** = adjective
A = article	**Adv** = adverb
Voc = vocabulary	**C** = countable noun
Sp = spelling	**U/C** = uncountable noun
P = punctuation	**Reph.** = rephrase
W W = wrong word	**ʌ** = missing word

Look at how the correction code is used in Text A, and see if you can correct the highlighted errors. Then use the code to mark the errors you find in Text B. There is one mistake in each line.

Text A

> A woman called in a repairman to mind her television, which was **Sp**
> in a magnificent cabinet. Just as he finish, the woman heard her **T**
> husband's key in the look. **Sp**
> 'Hurry!', she said to the repairman. 'You have to hide. My
> **Adj** husband is very jealously. There was no time to run out through the
> back door so the repairman hid into the television console. **WW**
> The husband came in and collapsed to watch some football on **WW**
> television into his favourite chair. The repairman was squashed and **WO**
> **Sp** getting hoter and hoter. Finally he can't stand it any more. He **P**
> **WW** climbed out, marched over the room and out of the front door.
> **ʌ** The husband looked the television set looked at his wife looked **P**
> back at the television set again and said I didn't see the referee send **P**
> **T** that chap off the field, do you? **P**

Text B

Haven't you forgotten something?

Tom Wilson is not the sort of chap who normally forget
things. A highly-respectable back manager, he has never
been stopped by the police, either. he was therefore
horrified when, driving along a quiet road last friday
evening, he heard sound of a police siren behind him.
Work at the bank had been worser than usual all week. Now
though, he was escaping to his house on the country, as he
at weekends always did. He sighed happily. He and his wife
had stoped at a little restaurant about an hour ago and the
tang of oysters was still on his lips. Today more then ever
before he is filled with a tremendous sense of peace and
tranquility as the countryside stretch out in front him.
Then the sirens interupt his dreams.
As the police cat overtook him, Tom's sense of horror
increased. Seated next to the driver was a women who was
the exactly picture of his wife. Was he going mad? Was it a
ghost? If so, the ghost looked flushed and angrily.
In confusion, Tom looked in the seat beside him. Then the
awful truth hit him he had left his wife behind at the
restaurant – and has never even noticed her absence!
'I thought it was a bit quite!' Tom remarked. 'My friends
think is hilarious. I am hoping my wife will see the funny
side of it all soon.' His wife, which is spending a few
day with her mother, has declined to comment.

The next time you do some writing, exchange your work with a partner
and check in the same way. With practice, you will find it much easier
to spot errors. In the examination, you need to write quickly and it is
easy to make mistakes. The editing skills you are practising now are
valuable examination techniques which will help you to spot errors in
your own work and correct them.

UNIT 1

Describing a person

1 Scan the text below. Where do you think it comes from – a letter, a report, a newspaper? Give reasons for your answer.

2 Look at paragraph one. The sentence in italics is the TOPIC SENTENCE. It tells us what the paragraph is about. The other sentences in the paragraph develop that topic. Choose topic sentences for the remaining paragraphs from the list below.

I Travelled with Kate Adie!

JANE HARDY REPORTS ON A SURPRISE MEETING
WITH A REMARKABLE JOURNALIST

I bumped into Kate Adie, BBC's top special correspondent, at Heathrow Airport last week. She had just checked in and was sitting quietly in the departure lounge, apparently unaware that her fellow passengers were pointing and staring at her with great interest. I saw her again just last night on the television, reporting from the middle of a war zone. With shells falling all round her, she looked just as cool and relaxed as she had in that airport lounge.

----------------------------- She is slim and fit-looking, with short blond hair and piercing, shrewd blue eyes. There is an air of confidence and toughness about her but also a hint of that deep intelligence and sensitivity which marks her style of reporting.

----------------------------- She normally wears trousers and shirts, often khaki, which blend in with the background in whatever disaster area or war zone she happens to be. Off duty, and for special occasions, she can look very elegant in stylish, though never outlandish, outfits.

----------------------------- Apart from the fact that

she is unmarried and has no children, little is known about her life away from work. Her interests and hobbies, such as they are, remain a mystery

----------------------------- She has succeeded in a field normally dominated by men, because she is the best. This is because she passionately believes in what she's doing and in reporting the truth, no matter how much courage it takes. Her precise, composed reporting from the world's disaster zones have made her one of the most respected women of the decade.

a Her clothes are always practical, as you would expect from someone who has to live out of suitcases.

b Kate has become a heroine to many thousands of television viewers.

c Physically, Kate Adie looks well equipped for the rigours of life as an international correspondent.

d She does not welcome questions about her personal life.

Useful adjectives

1 Look at these people. Would you like to be friends with them? What sort of people do you think they are? What do you imagine they do as a job/in their free time? What sort of music do you like? Use the words on page 9 (and your imagination!) to describe them.

She/He looks (quite) ...   He appears to be (rather) ...
I would imagine she is ...   I think he/she likes ...
I would guess he is ...

2   Which of the adjectives below could you use to describe yourself? Make a list and then see if your partner agrees with you!

lively/dull   shy/self-confident
quiet/talkative   ambitious/easy-going
reserved/outgoing   friendly/cold
dreamy/down to earth   kind/unsympathetic
serious/good fun   even-tempered/moody
adventurous/home-loving   cheerful/miserable
generous/self-centred

3   Can you add any more descriptive adjectives to the list? Write them down and compare your list with the rest of the class.

4   You are dreaming of your ideal girlfriend/boyfriend. What is he/she like? Add your ideas to the list.

Looks   **Personality**
blue eyes   exciting!
blond   not too sporty

Hyphenated adjectives

> *He's got a bad temper. – He's bad-tempered.*

Look at the box above, then change the following in the same way.

1   He's got dark hair.   4   She's got long legs.
2   She's got a quick temper.   5   She dresses well. (She's ...)
3   He's got round shoulders.   6   She's got blue eyes.

Order of adjectives

Notice the usual order of adjectives in a sentence:

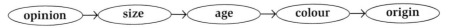

opinion → size → age → colour → origin

> *He was a cheerful, young, black American.*
> *She was a tall, long-legged, tanned Italian.*

9

If there is no other difference between the adjectives, we put the shortest one first:

> *a tall, long-legged girl*

Put the following adjectives in the correct order.

1 He was an /English/attractive/young/man.
2 She was a /little/teenage/boring/schoolgirl.
3 She is a /Colombian/hard-working/quiet/student.
4 She was dressed in a /full-length/stunning/Italian creation.
5 He's got /brown/beautiful/big/eyes.

Do not pack too many adjectives into one phrase, or it will seem more like a shopping list than a description! A list of three or four is probably the maximum for one phrase.

How good is your memory?

USEFUL PHRASES
You are ...   You've got ...
You're wearing ...

Stand back to back with your partner. Try to describe him/her accurately without turning round. Your partner will tell you if you are right or wrong as you go along.

Describing a person you knew in the past

Notice the use of tenses in this description of someone who is no longer alive.

> My grandfather **was** special. He **was** tall and bent with age but he **used to** climb our local mountain as easily as the wild goats that roamed the area. He **used to** love winter and as soon as the first snows arrived he **would** take us children to the wooden chalet up the mountain for a week's training in skiing and tobogganing!

Now describe a figure from the past in the same way.

Planning

Before you start to write a composition you need to gather your ideas. One way to do this is to 'brainstorm' ideas and make a spidergraph. You can then divide your ideas into paragraphs.

1 **Study this example and then complete the writer's paragraph plan for the 'Kate Adie' text on page 11.**

Clothes
trousers/shirts
stylish off-duty

Introduction
Who is she?
When/Where I saw her

KATE

Private life
a mystery
unmarried (no children)

Conclusion
Why I chose her
Why she's well known

Looks
slim
fit
blue eyes
blond

Personality
intelligent
sensitive
tough

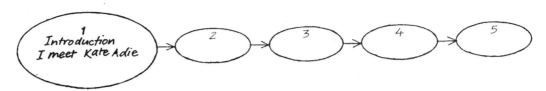

2 Why do you think the writer divided the paragraphs like this?

3 How does the writer make it clear that he/she has begun a new paragraph?

True or False?

When you write, it is very important that you divide your work into paragraphs.

Say if these questions are true or false to find out how much you already know about paragraphing.

1 Most compositions have two paragraphs.
2 Most compositions have a beginning, middle and end, so they need a minimum of three paragraphs.
3 Most paragraphs consist of just one line.
4 You start a new paragraph each time you begin a completely fresh topic.
5 Every paragraph should have a topic sentence.
6 The topic sentence introduces the topic of the paragraph.
7 The topic sentence is often the first sentence of the paragraph.

Written tasks

1 Imagine you have just started a new class and have met someone you really like. You are writing home. Write the part of the letter (2 or 3 paragraphs) in which you describe this person. Remember to begin each paragraph with a topic sentence.

2 Write an article for a class magazine entitled: *'The person I most admire'*. You could write about a famous person, a pop star, a member of your family – or even your teacher! Before you begin, draw a spidergraph, like the one you saw earlier in this Unit. Remember to divide your writing into paragraphs.

USEFUL TIPS

PLANNING

Before you start, make a spidergraph plan. Decide which ideas are important enough to include in your task and then group them under different headings. The headings will help you see when you should start a new paragraph.

STYLE/REGISTER

Look at the **Written tasks** again to check who is going to read your text and why. Make sure you choose the sort of language and the format they are expecting.

WORD ORDER

Check back to the rules about word order in descriptions that you saw in this Unit.

UNIT 2

A friendly letter

1 Cover the letter below. Can you answer these questions?

When you write a friendly/informal letter:
1 Where exactly should you put your address and the date?
2 Should you write your name at the top of the letter?
3 Do you need to put the address of the person you are writing to?
4 Where exactly should you write the salutation (Dear Sue, etc.)
5 Where should you start the first paragraph?
6 Should your letter contain more than one paragraph?

2 Now look at the model letter. Notice that the writer has indented each line, as is common in handwritten letters. Then answer the questions below.

16 O'Donnell Street
Castlebar
County Mayo
Ireland

16 June, 199-

Dear Sue,

It seems hard to believe that I've been here in Ireland for a whole week now! I promised to write and tell you how I was getting on – so here goes!

When I first got here, I just couldn't get used to the slow pace of life! Now, though, I'm learning to take things easy – and I'm beginning to feel really at home. My first impression of the Irish is that they are really, really friendly and helpful – and they certainly know how to enjoy life!

I've managed to rent a little cottage here in Castlebar. The countryside round about is marvellous – and very green because it rains a lot! I've already done some fishing and sailing and have made friends with some of the young people in the village. We spend most evenings in the local bar which has a real peat fire and great music – and Guinness too, of course!

Sorry this letter is so short but you know how bad I am at writing letters! Do write back when you have a spare minute. I miss you so much!

All my love,
Tom

1 Why is Tom writing this letter?
2 Who is going to read it?
3 What is their relationship, do you think?
4 What do you think Sue wants to know from the letter?
5 Does the letter tell her this?
6 Is the format and language appropriate for this sort of letter? Why?/Why not?
7 What is the topic of each of the paragraphs in Tom's letter?

Layout

A letter usually contains the following stages:

opening (Dear X)

↓

reasons for writing

↓

development

↓

closing remarks

↓

signature

You should use at least one paragraph for EACH of the stages.

Recent activities

Present Perfect or Past Simple? Use the prompts to write questions and then interview your partner.

Where/you/be/this week?
Where have you been this week?

1 You/be/out anywhere nice with friends? Where and when/go?
2 What/you/do/last weekend?
3 You/be/cinema/this week? What/see?
4 You/work hard/this week?
5 You/play/any sports recently? Where/play?

Discussion

Imagine you are spending three months abroad. This is your first week. Discuss these questions with your partner. Use your imagination! Make some notes, as you will need the ideas later.

How are you getting on? Are you homesick, do you think?
Who/What do you miss, apart from your family?
How did you feel when you first arrived?
What are your first impressions of the people/country?
What is the most difficult thing to get used to?
What is there to do – and what have you been doing recently?

Formal v Informal

Tom's letter is friendly, so the vocabulary and structures are informal. Always think about who you are writing to before you begin your letter. Mistakes in style make your letter look odd or even impolite.

Find the *friendly/informal* language in this list.

I have been here.
I've been here.
They're really, really friendly.
They are extremely friendly.
Thank you for your prompt attention to my letter.
Thanks a lot for writing back so soon.
I am writing to inform you that ...
Did you know that ...?
I would be extremely grateful if you could ...

Oh! I nearly forgot. Do you think you can ...?
You've really made my day!
You have been extremely helpful!
I have been very busy recently.
I've been up to my eyes in work.
By the way, I've just got to tell you that ...
Incidentally, I should also inform you that ...
I look forward to hearing from you as soon as possible.
Well must rush now. Write soon, won't you?

Punctuation – Capital letters and full stops

1 **Can you add three more examples to this list of rules for the use of capital letters?**

We use capital letters for:
a) beginnings of sentences
b) for the personal pronoun *I*
c) for names of people, streets and companies
d) for countries, nationalities, languages
e) for titles of books and films
f) for days of the week, months of the year

We use full stops to separate two complete sentences.

2 **Put capital letters, commas and full stops in this letter.**

dear ursula
thanks for your letter and the photos of the carnival last month i've just found out i'll be in london for a business meeting on wednesday it would be great if you could meet me for lunch
the meeting was only arranged today so i couldn't tell you sooner i do hope you can make it it seems ages since we last met up and i've got lots of news to give you please feel free to bring david along if he has the time
let me know as soon as you can and i'll book a table at our usual restaurant ring me tonight if you can
must dash now hope to hear from you soon
love
david

Remember! Good punctuation is important because it makes your writing clear and easy to read. Reading your text aloud can help too.

Vocabulary practice

Form adjectives from the following nouns.

friend – friendly

sympathy   reserve   help   kindness   rudeness
humour   impatience   happiness   loneliness

Written tasks

1   You are spending three months abroad. Complete this letter to an
English-speaking friend telling him/her about your experiences.
Look at the USEFUL TIPS below before you begin.

....

....

....

Dear .... ,
    Well, here I am in .... ! I arrived here ....
    When I first arrived, I found ....
....
    I've done quite a lot since I've been here. ....
....
....
    ....

2   Write a letter to an English-speaking friend inviting him/her to come
to your house and have a holiday with you. Tell him/her about the
local countryside, and the people. Suggest how you could spend the
time together. Look at the USEFUL TIPS below before you begin. Plan
the layout of your letter before you start.

USEFUL LANGUAGE
I wonder if you'd like to ...   How about ...?
We could ...   I think you'd enjoy ...
Let me know if ...

USEFUL TIPS
LAYOUT
Check with the model letter that you remember how to lay out a friendly letter
correctly.
PARAGRAPHS
Group your sentences into paragraphs. Start a new paragraph for each
complete change of subject. Make sure you have a key sentence for each
paragraph, which summarises the theme of the paragraph. Remember to start
each new paragraph on a new line.
REGISTER/STYLE
You are writing to a friend so remember to use informal language.
TENSES
Remember that you can use the Present Perfect to talk about recent activities.

UNIT 3

A formal letter

1 **Cover the letter below and answer these questions.**

In a **formal** letter, where do you put:
your address?
your name?
the number of your house?
the date?
the address of the person you are writing to?

In a **formal** letter, do you usually:
use contractions (*I'm, They'd*)?
need to use paragraphs?
put your name at the top?
address strangers as *Sir* or *Madam*?

2 **Now look at John's letter and check if you were right. Notice that the writer has used blocked style, as is common in typed letters.**

```
                                        17 Enfield Road
                                        Twickenham
                                        Middlesex
                                        TW6 7JY
                                        August 6 199-


Quality Leathers
112 Castle Road
Edinburgh
ED8 7HP


Dear Sir,
I am writing to complain about a leather jacket which I bought from your
store while on holiday three weeks ago. I tried a jacket on in the shop
and checked it carefully for flaws. When I got to the cash desk, however,
the assistant persuaded me to take one which was already packaged, and
assured me it was perfect.
When I got home and tried the jacket on, I found a large rip under the
side pocket. As you will realise, I was extremely upset to discover this.
The jacket was by no means cheap, and I only bought it from you because
of your reputation for quality. In fact I have always recommended your
store to friends in the past. I shall think twice before I do so again!

I am returning the jacket with this letter and look forward to receiving
an apology and a full refund of the cost — £290.50.

I look forward to hearing from you,
Yours faithfully,

John Hull

John HULL
```

3 **Why is John writing this letter? Who is going to read it? What does John hope their reaction will be? Is the format and language of the letter appropriate for this? Why?/Why not?**

4 **What is the topic of each of the paragraphs?**

Making complaints

Look at the pictures and match the items below.

1	The book	a	was missing.
2	The hairdryer	b	was dented.
3	The CD	c	was torn.
4	The wheel	d	was faulty.
5	The sweater	e	was scratched.
6	The zip	f	was unwound.
7	A piece of the puzzle	g	was faded.
8	The cassette	h	was stuck.

Describing objects

Notice the usual order of descriptive adjectives in a sentence:

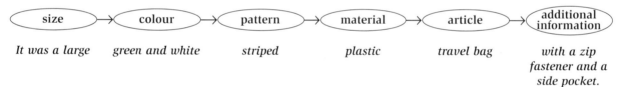

size	colour	pattern	material	article	additional information
It was a large	*green and white*	*striped*	*plastic*	*travel bag*	*with a zip fastener and a side pocket.*

1 Put one of your possessions (e.g. your bag) on the table. Imagine you lost it! Describe it to the person next to you.

2 Now describe the articles in the pictures. Use the language in the box to help you.

USEFUL LANGUAGE
leather/plastic/woollen/polyester/cotton
with a long/short strap
with a buckle/pop fastener/zip
with my initials/name on it
with a sticker/badge on it

Relative pronouns

> I am writing to complain about a jacket. I bought it in your store.
> *I am writing to complain about a jacket **which I bought in your store.***
>
> I gave it to the shop assistant. She assured me it was perfect.
> *I gave it to the shop assistant **who assured me it was perfect.***
>
> I did not buy the jacket. I had tried it on.
> *I did not buy **the jacket I had tried on.***

Look at the examples. Then join the following sentences in the same way. Omit the relative pronoun where possible.

1 I spoke to the assistant. She was here yesterday.
2 She gave me a credit note. It was not what I expected.
3 The sum was not right. It was written on the cheque.
4 I showed him the letter. I had put it in my pocket.

Starting and ending a formal letter

a
Dear Miss White,
....
Best wishes

b
Dear Mr Collins,
....
Yours sincerely,

Look at the skeleton letters below. Which format (a, b, c or d), would you use to write to:

your teacher?
your close friend?
the manager of your bank?
(you do not know his/her name)
the manager of a company?

c
Dear Sam,
....
Love,

d
Dear Sir,
....
Yours faithfully,

Organising your letter

In this letter, the paragraphs are jumbled. With your partner, decide on the right order. The words in italics link the original text together.

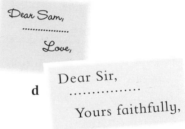

159 Saxby Street
Leicester
LC6 5PG
November 16 199-

Marks and Spencer,
Oxford St.,
London
WC1 3BT

Dear Sir/Madam,

a Please could you let me know if anybody has handed in a watch *of this description,* and if it would be possible to have it *sent* to me.

b I will, of course, send on the *cost of postage* if necessary. Otherwise, I will be in town again in two week's time and could pick it up then.

c *It* is a gold watch with a square face and a cream leather strap. It also has my initials, J.E. on the back, enclosed in a little heart. I am desperate to find it because it was a present from my boyfriend.

d I am writing to ask if anyone has handed in *a gold watch* which I think I lost in your store last Saturday morning. I took it off to try on a bracelet, and then probably left it on the counter.

I look forward to hearing from you.

Yours faithfully,
Jan Edwards
Jan Edwards

Useful phrases

These phrases are commonly used in formal letters.

Thank you for your letter of ...
I am writing in reply to ...
I am writing to inform you of ...
        to complain about ...
        to enquire about ...
        to apply for ...
        for more information about ...
I would be grateful if you could/would ...
Could you possibly ...
I would be grateful if you would ...
I look forward to hearing from you/ meeting you very soon.

Puncuation - using commas 1

We use commas:

a) to divide groups of words in a sentence so that the meaning is clear.

> *He got up, dressed, had breakfast and shaved.*

b) to seperate items in lists.

> *She was tall, blonde, witty and evil.*

Do not use a comma to link two seperate sentences together. In this case, you must use a full stop.

Written tasks

1 **You have been sent a gift for Christmas but there is something wrong with it. Write to the shop to complain. First make a plan of what you are going to write and show your teacher. Be careful with commas!**

2 **While staying at a large hotel you lost something valuable. Write a letter to the hotel manager, desciding what you lost and where you might have left it. Make a plan first. Be careful with commas!**

USEFUL TIPS

LAYOUT
Look back to the model letter in this Unit to check you know how to lay out a formal letter.

PARAGRAPHS
Try to link the sentences in each paragraph, and the paragraphs themselves.

STYLE/REGISTER
Remember that you are writing to a stranger. Make sure your language is formal.

LANGUAGE
Look again at the rules on word order and the descriptive vocabulary you met in this Unit.

Transactional letter–Applying for holiday jobs

1 Look at the advertisement below. Would you be interested in a job like this? What would you want to know about it before you decided to take it? What might the drawbacks be?

2 If you wanted the job, what would you say about yourself in your letter? How formal do you think your letter should be?

HOLIDAY JOBS!

Need to improve your English?
Want to spend some time abroad?
Short of cash?

Why not come and work for us at
Home Farm!

You'll be picking fruit and generally helping out with all the usual farm work. We'll pay you by the hour so the harder you work, the more you'll
earn! We'll provide a place to sleep and all your meals.

Interested? Why not drop us a line (and a photo). We'll be happy to answer any queries.

Mr and Mrs Bull, Cold Comfort Farm, Sussex, Great Britain SU3 8TZ

Michel Dupont saw the advertisement and made these notes.

QUESTIONS TO ASK
When does the job start and finish?
Will I be the only one there?
Where exactly will I sleep?
What is the minimum rate per hour?
How many hours will I be expected to work?
Can I have a photo of the farm?

3 Scan the letter below. Do you think the farmer would be satisfied with it? Why?/Why not? Now answer the questions.

Rue Vichy
Troyes
France

16 May, 199-

Dear Mr and Mrs Bull,

I saw your advertisement in the paper and am very interested in working on your farm.

I'm a student and need more practice with my English. I was hoping to come to Great Britain but didn't want to ask my parents for money. Working for you would be an ideal solution.

I am 18 years old and very fit. Although I've never worked on a farm before I have helped on a building site and am used to working hard. I'm very fond of animals and would be happy to help with the cows and sheep if needed.

Could you please let me know how long you would want me for, how many hours a day, and what the minimum wages per hour would be. I would like to know if there will be other students there too and where I will be sleeping.

I enclose a photo as requested. My last employer will be happy to write me a reference, if you so wish.

I look forward to hearing from you soon,

Yours sincerely,

Michel Dupont

1 Has Michel given the information he was asked for in the advertisement? Has he asked about all the points he noted down himself?
2 The advertisement was informal – is Michel's letter
   a) too formal?
   b) too informal?
   c) just right?
3 Has Michel used clear paragraphs for each new section of the letter? How does he show he is beginning a new paragraph?

Comparing texts

Mr and Mrs Bull received another letter on the same day but they were not very impressed! Why?

> Paris
> Tuesday, 16 May
>
> Dear Sir/Madam,
> I saw your advertisement in the newspaper and am quite interested at the job. I'm 16, a student, and I really want a holiday away from the parents. I'm fit and healthy and I adore to be outdoors. The only problem is that I'm scared from cows but I could keep away from them, I expect?
> Please tell me how much I earn exactly and what there is to do in the evenings. No discos, I suppose?
> My friend Daniel, who goes to college with me, would also like a job. Could you let me know if you need any more helpers?
> I am sending the only photo I have at the moment, but please don't worry. My leg will be out of plaster soon.
>
> Please write back soon!
>
> Regards, Didier

Spot the error

Didier's letter contains errors in each of the areas below. Find examples of each type and underline them.

– structure (grammar)
– layout
– inappropriate greeting
– inappropriate ending
– paragraphing
– inappropriate language (too formal or too informal)
– inappropriate content
– style inconsistent (changes from formal to informal)

Planning

Look back to Michel's letter and complete this plan.

1 Opening → 2 → 3 → 4 → 5

Vocabulary – Work

Check that you know the meaning of the words below. Then complete the blanks in the text with an appropriate word.

applicant(s)	interview	dismissed
apply	salary	redundancy
application	wages	redundant
application form	employer	retirement
CV	employee	pension
referee	promotion	
reference	fired	

When a friend told me that one of the ..... at his bank
had been ..... for stealing, I decided to ..... for the
job. I filled in the ..... form, asked my last boss for
a ..... and wrote a ..... detailing my experience and
qualifications.
Fortunately, I was selected for an ..... . On the big
day, I waited with five other nervous ..... and then it
was my turn. The manager outlined the job, the I
would earn, and prospects for ..... . I am pleased to
say that she is now my new ..... .

Linking words

Notice how we join two contradictory sentences. Look carefully at the punctuation.

He's a good salesman. He has no qualifications.

*He has no qualifications **but** he is a good salesman.*
***Although** he has no qualifications, he is a good salesman.*
***In spite of having** no qualifications, he is a good salesman.*
***In spite of the fact that** he has no qualifications, he is a good salesman.*
*He has no qualifications. **Nevertheless**, he is a good salesman.*
*He has no qualifications. **However**, he is a good salesman.*

Join these sentences in each of the ways shown above.

1   I failed the exams. I still want to be a vet.
2   He is the manager's son. He was fired.
3   They are millionaires. They work ten hours a day.

Gerund or Infinitive?

Complete the sentences with the preposition and the correct form of the verb.

1   I would like ..... (*work*) with animals.
2   I am interested ..... (*find*) work abroad.
3   My last employer advised me ..... (*write*) to you.
4   Unfortunately, I am unable ..... (*start*) work until November.
5   I am looking forward ..... (*hear*) from you.
6   I enjoy ..... (*deal*) with the public.

Writing for information

1 Read the advertisement below and the written notes which accompany it.

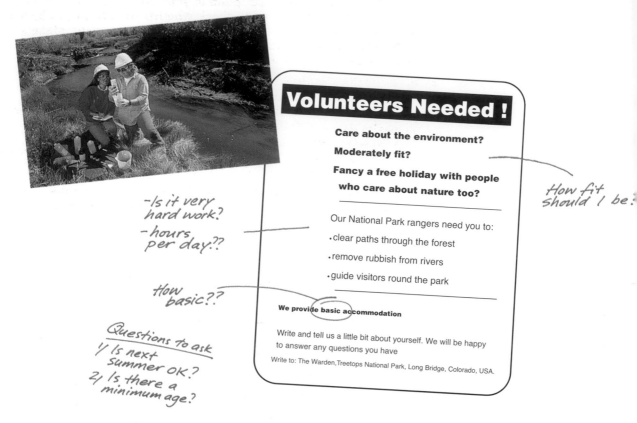

- Is it very hard work?
- hours per day.??

How basic??

How fit should I be?

Questions to ask
1/ Is next summer OK.?
2/ Is there a minimum age?

Volunteers Needed !

Care about the environment?

Moderately fit?

Fancy a free holiday with people who care about nature too?

Our National Park rangers need you to:
- clear paths through the forest
- remove rubbish from rivers
- guide visitors round the park

We provide basic accommodation

Write and tell us a little bit about yourself. We will be happy to answer any questions you have

Write to: The Warden, Treetops National Park, Long Bridge, Colorado, USA.

2 **Now discuss the following questions with a partner.**

1 Are you interested in natural history?
2 Do you worry about environmental problems (like pollution) or do you think the subject is not important or even boring?
3 Would you volunteer for a holiday like the one above? Why?/Why not?
4 What other questions would you want to ask if you wrote for information?
5 What sort of person do you think the advertisers are looking for? What sort of letter are they expecting – formal or informal? Underline the important points in the advertisement that you should refer to when you write to volunteer.

USEFUL LANGUAGE

I saw your advertisement in ...
I would like to apply for a job as ...
I would like to know more about ...
Please could you send me details about ...
Could you please let me know ...
I am sending a photograph/a reference as requested.
I can come for an interview at any time.
I look forward to hearing from you.

Written tasks

1 You are thinking of volunteering to work in Treetops National Park for a week next summer. You are planning to write a letter to the warden, giving a brief description of yourself and asking for more information. You will need to check whether the period you have in mind is suitable. Look at the notes on the advertisement. Make a spidergraph plan of what you are going to write, and number the ideas in the order you will write them in the letter.

2 a) Write the first draft of your letter to Treetops National Park. Before you start, think about who you are writing to and why. Will your letter be formal or informal? How should you address it?

b) Exchange your draft of the letter to Treetops with a partner. Check each other's work, looking especially at punctuation, spelling and paragraphing. Tell each other about any errors. Then write a second draft of your letter.

3 You are interested in the job below. Write a letter giving the information requested and including any queries you have.

Do you like having fun?
Do you want to be with young people?
Can you organise sports and entertainments?
Have you had experience of camping?
Can you cook?

Volunteers Needed at
SUMMER CAMPS!

We need helpers for our youth camps in the USA this summer.
Accommodation and modest salary provided.

Interested? Write and tell us a little about yourself. Send your letter to:

Samba Youth Camps
2214 Creek Drive Colorado USA

P.S.   Need more information?
Just send us your queries with your letter and we will write back immediately!

USEFUL TIPS

PLANNING
Underline the important points in an advertisement before you reply, and keep checking back as you write to make sure you have included all the relevant points.

PARAGRAPHING
Remember to group your ideas into paragraphs and to start each paragraph on a new line, preferably indented. A paragraph should normally contain more than one sentence!

STYLE
Decide how formal your letter should be before you start writing. Make sure the style is consistent throughout your letter.

UNIT 5

Writing a narrative

1 Before you read the extract, think about the following questions.

1 How often have you travelled by air? Do you enjoy it?
2 Have you ever had any interesting/frightening experiences while flying?

In this story, written for her school magazine, Maria Klein explains why she will never fly again.

The Most Frightening Day Of My Life

I was so excited when I was selected to play basketball for my country. We were to fly to the USA, and, as I drove to the airport, I kept thinking how luck seemed to be going so much my way these days. The sun was blazing down – just the right sort of day for flying, or so I thought.

I met the other members of my basketball team at the airport. There were thirteen of us on the flight. We were laughing and joking as the plane taxied down the runway. Nobody took much notice of the safety video they were showing. After all, we'd seen it all before – and wasn't flying the safest way to travel?

The plane was completing its ascent when we heard an explosion! There was a terrible hush. Then, a whisper of panic went round the plane. A frightened-looking steward appealed for calm. He was still speaking when, suddenly, the front of the plane seemed to dip and we realised we were hurtling towards the ground!

I suppose it all lasted only a few minutes, but to me it was a lifetime. People around me shouted and screamed, but I just felt numb with disbelief. Was this really the end of everything?

Then, against all hope, we felt the plane level out and we slowly began to gain height. As everyone cheered, the pilot announced that he had the situation under control. We made an emergency landing a few minutes later.

Two years on, experts still haven't revealed the cause of the incident. Until they do, I will never take another flight. In fact, to be honest, I don't think I will ever fly again. It was the most frightening experience of my life – and one that I do not mean to repeat!

2 Now answer the following questions.

1 Who are the intended readers of this story? Why is the author writing the story – to inform, persuade, interest, or frighten her readers? Does she succeed in doing this? If so, how?
2 Do you think the first paragraph provides a good opening to the story? Why?/Why not?
3 The writer uses some quite short sentences in Paragraph 3. What is the effect of varying the length of sentences in a text?
4 In what other ways does the writer make the story exciting?

Planning

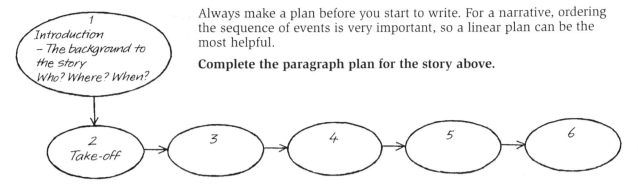

Always make a plan before you start to write. For a narrative, ordering the sequence of events is very important, so a linear plan can be the most helpful.

Complete the paragraph plan for the story above.

To write a good story you need to do these things:

- Catch the reader's attention by making the beginning of your story dramatic or unusual. The first paragraph should set the scene, *and* make the reader interested enough to want to read on!
- Plan the sequence of events carefully. Events should follow each other in a logical order.
- Start a new paragraph for each new stage of the story. This makes your story easier to read. Leave a clear gap between paragraphs.
- Leave yourself time to write a good ending. There is nothing worse than reading an exciting story that just stops in mid air!

Narrative tenses

1 Look at the story again. How many past tense forms can you find? Can you say why they are used?

2 Match the items below and find one example of each in the text.

1	Use the Past Continuous tense (*was ....ing*)	A	to show one action was finished *before* another began
2	Use the Past Perfect (*had done/had been doing*)	B	to describe what happened *after* the main event began OR to list a sequence of separate events
3	Use the Past Simple	C	to paint the background – to describe what was happening *at the same time as* the main event began

3 Study the three pictures below. They show what happened on a beach in Brazil last year, when there was a shark attack! Then discuss the questions below with a partner.

1   How often do you go swimming in the sea? Are you afraid of deep water?
2   Which sea creatures are dangerous? What do you know about sharks?

Painting the background to a story

Complete this paragraph, which describes the events in picture 1 (*before* the attack). Use the Past Continuous, Past Simple and Past Perfect tense.

I remember everything vividly! We had just arrived at my favourite beach. It was just an ordinary summer afternoon and the beach was crowded. People ....(sunbathe) or ....(get out) the picnic things, ready for lunch. Some kids ....(already/mark out) a football pitch in the sand with piles of clothes and were now in the middle of an exciting game. Others ....(swim) or ....(paddle). An ice-cream man ....(park) on the sand sometime before and he ....(do) excellent business. There was a surfing competition going on, and I ....(watch) the brown bodies of the surfers ride the waves. Then I ....(hear) a voice scream 'Shark! Shark!'.

Describing the main events

In pairs, complete the next paragraph of the story, which describes what happened *after* the shark was seen.

Exchange your version with another group. Check the tenses are correct, then decide who has written the most dramatic version. (Say why!)

At first everything seemed very quiet. Then, everyone started to .... and .... They watched in horror as .... The people in the water .... and .... Parents .... One of the children .... Seconds later, the coast guard arrived and .... The onlookers held their breath! The shark ....

Punctuation – Using commas

You need commas to separate groups of words from each other and make your text easier to read.

Use commas:

a) for words that give us extra information but can be left out:

> *The kids, **who had marked out a football pitch**, were now in the middle of a match.*
> *My sister, **a nurse at a big hospital**, comforted the children.*
> *She was, **however**, unable to do much to help.*

b) when you begin a sentence with a subordinate clause:

> *If I saw a shark, I would die!*
> *Although I can't swim, I love the sea.*

Proofreading

This is the first part of a story about a fire. In each line of the text, there is a word which should not be there. Underline the word.

The last year I spent my summer holidays in a popular
resort on the Mediterranean coast. The hotel it was
comfortable and the weather was perfect! In the fact, I was
having a marvellous holiday until was the fire!
It was the Saturday evening and everybody was relaxing in
the lounge or disco, were tired after a long day on the
beach. The disco it was on the ground floor of the hotel and
this particular Saturday at night it was crowded with
people dancing and drinking. A disc jockey he was playing
music from the 60s and people were singing with along
and having a good time. It was then we did saw the smoke!

Paragraph jumble

1 The sentences in the next paragraph of the story are in the wrong order. Write them out correctly.

One of these exits was locked, **however**, so people were forced to turn back and join the crowds at the other exits. **Then,** black smoke began to fill the room, and the shrill sound of the fire bell rang out. **Finally,** as the last person left the building, we heard the sound of the fire engines arriving. For a moment, **confused by the unfamiliar sound,** nobody moved. **At first,** only a few people noticed the fire. A **few seconds later,** coughing and choking, everybody raced towards their nearest fire exits.

2 Did the words in bold help you to put the text in order? If so, how?

Linking words

Linking words improve the style of your text. The words below are useful for listing a sequence of events.

Can you add any more words to the list? (Include examples from the text you have just read.)

In the beginning, ...	After that, ... A few seconds/ minutes/ later, ... A while later, ...	In the end, ...

Punctuation

The final paragraph of the story is difficult to read because the writer has used almost no punctuation.

Put punctuation marks and capital letters in the story where necessary. (If you find this difficult, try reading the text to a partner. This should help you see where you need commas and full stops.)

The firemen who had arrived very quickly fought their way into the building and eventually got the fire under control luckily nobody was seriously hurt the holiday company offered us rooms in another hotel nearby but my holiday was spoilt i packed my bags and flew home the next day While I have been to other discos since then I never really enjoy them that really was the most frightening experience of my life!

Discussion

It is often easiest to write a story based on personal experience. Stop and think! *What was the most exciting* or *the most enjoyable* or *the most frightening day of your life?*

Now talk to a partner about that experience, using the prompts below.

1 *Ask about the background.*
   When/happen? Where/be/you? Anyone/with you? What/you/do/at the time?
2 *Ask about the event itself.*
   What/happen? How/you/feel? What/you/do/next? What/other people/do? What/happen/afterwards?
3 *Ask about later developments.*
   How/you/feel now, when/remember/this event? You/ever/dream about it? It/change/your life/any way?

Written tasks

1 You have been asked to write a story in English for your class magazine. Possible titles are: *'The most exciting experience of my life'* or *'The most enjoyable experience of my life'*. Write the story, using the ideas you gathered in the DISCUSSION exercise above. Before you begin, think who you are writing for and what you want them to feel as they are reading your story! Then choose a suitable style. Remember to make a plan before you begin.

2 You have to write a story for your class magazine beginning: *'I was just dropping off to sleep when I heard the sound of breaking glass'*. Work with a partner to plan your story. When you have finished your plan, write the story together. Before you begin, think who you are writing for and what you want them to feel as they are reading your story!

3 An English magazine is running a writing competition. The prize is a holiday in South Africa! You have to write a story ending with the words: *'I am happy to say I have never had that dream again'*.

Make a plan, then write your entry for the competition. Remember who you are writing for and why!

USEFUL TIPS

THINK OF YOUR READER

Always keep in mind who you are writing for and why. Ask yourself what your reader wants to know and how you want them to feel as they are reading. This will help you choose the right style and approach to your story.

PLANNING

Make a clear plan before you begin to write. A linear plan is most helpful for this. It will help you to describe events in the right order and help you to paragraph correctly.

TENSES

Remember that the Past Continuous and Past Perfect tense are used to paint the background to a story. Use the Past Simple to list events.

LINKING

Try to link your sentences together, as you practised in this Unit.

UNIT 6

Transactional letter – Making complaints

1 Before you read the advertisement, think about the following questions.

1 Describe the best holiday you have ever had. (Where was it? Who did you go with? What did you do/see?)

2 Has anything ever gone wrong while you were on holiday? (Have you ever lost or forgotten something? Have you been ill? Have you had problems with travel or hotels?)

The Wilson family had a lot of serious problems with their last holiday.

2 Read the advertisement they saw before they booked the holiday and look at Mrs Wilson's photos and comments. Check any vocabulary problems before you go on.

True!

- can they offer us another weekend at discount?
- will village be quiet?
- can we have accommodation in new block?
- if not, money back?

WALKING WEEKENDS IN SPECTACULAR SCENERY

- Escape city life for the peace of the mountains!
- Based in tranquil village
- Accommodation in new purpose-built block or in annexe
- Expert guide

new road!

The scenery was lovely.

Mrs Wilson notes

See our photo!

damp and cold!!

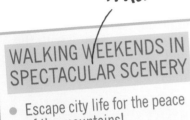

We heard the purpose-built block was lovely.

She had sprained her ankle.

They were building a new road through the village.

3 Now answer the following questions.

1 What do you think the family liked about the holiday? What was wrong with it? Where would they have preferred to sleep?

2 Look at Mrs Wilson's notes. Do the family want to repeat the holiday? On what conditions? What do they want if this is not possible?

Choosing a style

Mrs Wilson is going to write to the holiday company to explain why they are disappointed and to ask for another holiday or a refund.

Answer the following questions.

1 Should her letter be formal or informal?
2 How will she address the letter?
3 Which of the phrases below might she use? Which are the formal ones?

I am writing to you about our recent holiday.
You know we went on holiday with you last year? Well, ...
I'm so fed up I could scream!
I am feeling extremely disappointed.
Honestly, you should have seen our room!
Just look at these photos. I've got a point, haven't I?
If you look at the photographs, I am sure you will agree with me.
I would be grateful if you could ...
Could you ... ? I'd be ever so grateful!
Give me a refund, please.
I am sure you will agree that I should have a refund.
I'm dying to hear from you.
I look forward to hearing from you in the near future.

Drafting and redrafting

Remember that nobody writes perfectly on their first attempt. It is important to get used to rewriting and editing (checking) your work. Maybe you can persuade a friend to help you check!

1 **This is a draft of the letter Mrs Wilson is going to send. She has checked everything except capital letters and punctuation mistakes (there are quite a few!). Find them and correct them.**

1 Queens Court
london
WC4 7PB
27 april 199-

The Manager,
Country Breaks
Inverness IV4 6NP

dear sir/madam,
`Walking Weekend' April 24-26
my family and I have just returned from a weekend break in scotland, organised by your company *unfortunately* we have a number of complaints to make *when we arrived* we were shocked to find that a new road was being built through the village. we were *even more* upset *when* we saw our rooms. We were in the annexe and my son's room was damp and we were all frozen. *the next day* we met our guide. She was extremely nice *but* had twisted her ankle. We *therefore* had to keep our walks short *and* could not take advantage of the beautiful paths up the mountains. We **did** think the scenery was stunning, and would like to try another weekend *provided* the village is quiet and we can stay in the new block would you be willing to offer us a discount if we did *this*. *If not* i think you will agree that we should have a full refund on our holiday
I look forward to hearing from you,

N Wilson (Mrs)

2 Check your answers, then complete these punctuation rules.

1 You use a capital letter for .....
2 You use a full stop to .....
3 You use a comma .....
4 You use 's to show .....

3 Look at Mrs Wilson's letter again and answer the following questions.

1 How many paragraphs does she use?
2 What is the topic of each of the paragraphs?
3 How does she make it clear which holiday she is referring to at the beginning of the letter?
4 Are the format and language she uses appropriate for this task? Give examples.
5 Complete this spidergraph plan of her letter, and then number the ideas in the order she lists them in the letter.

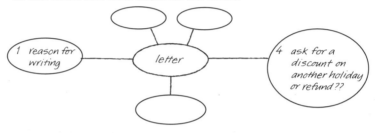

Linking words

Look at Mrs Wilson's letter again. It is easy to read because the ideas/sentences are linked together well. The words that help to link the text are in italics.

Here is another letter on the same subject. Work with a partner to choose the most suitable linking words.

Dear Sir/Madam,

Last week I went on one of your 'Walking Weekend' breaks in Scotland. **Unfortunately,** I **In spite of this,** **Therefore,**

was not at all satisfied with the holiday. **To start with** I was very disappointed with the **At first,**

village. It was extremely noisy **as** they were building a new road right through the **so** **owing to**

centre. I was **so** **thus** unable to sleep after 5.30 a.m. any morning. **Plus** when I was **though** **Added to this**

shown to my room, I found that **although** I had asked for a private bathroom, I had **because** **in spite of**

nowhere to wash at all. **At last** I really must mention the guide. **Because of** an **Eventually** **In spite of** **Last but not least**

accident the day before, she was unable to walk properly, so we could not do some of the marvellous walks I had been looking forward to.
I hope you agree that the weekend was not as advertised, and look forward to receiving compensation.
Yours faithfully

Sam Clark

Sam Clark

Planning

You have just come back from a holiday abroad. There were a number of things you were not happy about. Here are some photographs you took during the holiday, and a few points you noted down.

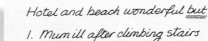

Hotel and beach wonderful <u>but</u>

1. Mum ill after climbing stairs every day.

2. Kids fed up because couldn't swim in pool.

3. Minibus broke down <u>3</u> times.

You are going to write a letter complaining about what went wrong on the holiday and asking for a refund of some of the money you paid or another holiday.

Make a spidergraph plan of what you are going to write and number the ideas in the order you will deal with them in the letter. Then look at WRITTEN TASKS 1.

Written tasks

1 Write the first draft of a letter to the holiday company using the plan you made earlier. The company is:
Luxury Tours, 221 Oxford Street, London WC1 6NG

Before you start, think who you are writing to and why. Will your letter be formal or informal? How should you address it?

2 Exchange your draft of the letter to Luxury Tours with a partner. Check each other's work, looking especially at punctuation, spelling and paragraphing. Tell each other about any errors. You might like to check with your teacher, too. Then write a second draft of your letter.

USEFUL TIPS

PLANNING

Always make a plan before you start, as you have practised in this Unit. Make sure you number the items in your plan too, so that your writing is logical and well-ordered.

STYLE

Remember that before you write any letter, it is important to stop and think **who** you are writing to and **why**.
In this Unit you are writing to a company so your language should be polite and formal.

LINKING WORDS

Your writing will be much better if you link your sentences together. Try to use the connectors you practised in this Unit.

UNIT 7 — Telling a story

1 Before you read the extract, think about the following questions.

1 Do you believe in life after death? And in ghosts?
2 Have you read or heard any good ghost stories? Can you tell one now?

2 Read the story below. As you read, think why the author is writing (to give facts, to persuade, to scare the reader). How does this affect the way she writes?

CROSSING OVER

If she hadn't been fond of dogs, she would never have volunteered for this particular job. When her class at school were asked if they would give up some of their spare time towards helping old people, most of the tasks on offer sounded dreary. ... But walking old Mrs Matthew's dog, that had seemed like something she might even enjoy.

What she hadn't reckoned with was the dog himself. ... He seemed to have no training and he certainly had no manners. He never stopped when she told him to, never came when she called him, so that every Saturday, when she let him run free among the bushes and little trees on the Common, she was afraid she might have to return to Mrs Matthews without the dog, confessing that he had run away.

This particular evening was horrible. She'd been kept later at school than usual, and although it was already March, the sky was overcast, it was beginning to get dark, and a fine rain made the pavements slippery. Togo was in a worse mood than usual. He was too strong for her to control, and he knew it.

They reached the zebra crossing on the hill. The traffic was moving fast, as it always did during the evening rush-hour. She stood still and dragged at Togo's lead. But Togo did not mean to be dictated to by a schoolgirl, and after a moment's hesitation, he pulled too. He was off, in the middle of the on-coming traffic. She threw all her weight against his, but she was no match for him. She thought she felt the worn leather snap, she heard the sound of screaming brakes and someone shouted.

She found herself standing on the further side of the road. ... She saw the bonnet of a red car crumpled by its contact with the back of a large yellow van. She saw, too, a dark stain on the road surface. Blood.

... She turned away from the accident and began to walk, on legs that trembled, up the hill towards her own home. She thought, 'I'll go and tell Mum.' But then she remembered how much Mrs Matthews loved horrible Togo, ... and how dreadful it was going to be for her to open her front door to find a policeman telling her that her dog was dead. She had to go first to Mrs Matthew's house to break the news gently. ...

Her heart beat furiously as she unlatched the small wooden gate and walked the short distance up to the front door, rehearsing exactly how to say what she had to. She lifted the knocker. ...

Extraordinary. From the other side of the door, she heard something very much like Togo's deep, menacing growl. She must be in such a state of nerves that she was imagining impossible things.

When Mrs Matthews looked out, she behaved in a very peculiar way. Instead of saying immediately, 'Where's Togo?' she asked nothing of her visitor, but bent forward and peered out, looking up and down the short row of cottages. ... Her head with its thinning grey hair was so close that the girl stepped back, opening her mouth to begin her explanation. But what she saw in the passage behind the old woman stopped her from uttering a sound.

At the further end of the passage was a dog. Togo. Togo, whole, apparently unharmed, his collar round his neck, and the end of the broken leash still attached, dragging behind him.

For a moment she thought he was going to spring forward and attack her. He was making a curious noise, not a howl, nor a growl, but a sort of whine. She noticed that he was trembling. ...

She started to speak. But Mrs Matthews appeared not to have heard her. She was turning back to calm the terrified dog. She was saying, 'Whatever's the matter with you, Togo? Think you're seeing a ghost?'

3 Now answer the following questions.

1 Is this a good ghost story? Why?/Why not?
2 Look at the title of the story. It has two possible meanings. Can you guess what they are?

More about paragraphing

Remember that to write well, you need clear paragraphs. These make the text easier for the reader to follow. You should start a new paragraph for each new aspect of the story or topic.

1   **What is the topic of each of the paragraphs in the model?**

2   **A paragraph usually has one central idea. This is summarised in the key sentence, which is often near the beginning of the paragraph. The other sentences explain or expand on this key sentence. Underline some of the key sentences in the text.**

3   **Good writers may vary the length of sentences in a paragraph. Find examples of very short sentences in the story. Why does the writer vary the length in this way? What effect does it have on the reader?**

Vocabulary

A good range of vocabulary is essential in story telling.

Complete the sentences with the best choice of verb. Remember to change the tense, if necessary.

1   *stroll, rush, go, walk*
    The dog ran off and she ..... after it, desperate to catch it before another car came.

2   *peer, gaze, stare, look*
    The woman ..... out at her through the cracked and misty glass.

3   *speak, scream, whisper, say*
    The girl ..... her secret quietly in her boyfriend's ear.

4   *laugh, giggle, chuckle, guffaw*
    The girls ..... helplessly as their teacher tripped over his bag.

First paragraphs

The first paragraph of your text is very important. If it is good, the reader will want to go on. If it is weak, he/she may give up!

1   **Look at these first paragraphs. Which make you want to read on? Why?**

It was midnight when the train shuddered to a halt. Anna and her sister woke up with a jump to find they were the only passengers left on the train. They stumbled onto the platform, into dense fog. The place was dark and deserted, wrapped in an eerie silence. Where was their taxi? They looked around uneasily as they waited ... and waited.

It was a nice day. The sun was shining and the birds were singing. Tom and Mario were excited. They were going on holiday to Italy. They were looking forward to swimming in the sea and walking in the hills.

'Keep driving. For Heaven's sake, keep driving!' I put my foot on the accelerator and the car leapt forward as the traffic lights changed to green. The woman in the back of the car crouched down in fear and started to cry. But who was she — and what was she doing in my car?

As you see, in the first paragraph of a story, you can awaken the reader's imagination by using a dramatic situation or a dialogue to set the scene.

2   Your teacher has asked you to plan a story based on the pictures above. Write the *first paragraph only*. You may like to work with a partner for this. When you have finished, compare what you have written with other students in your class.

Planning

You now have to plan what to write for the next part of the story. As you will probably want to relate the events in sequence, a linear plan like the one below will probably be best.

Complete the linear plan. (You can make it shorter or longer if necessary.)

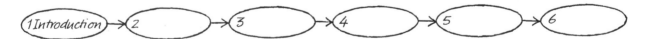

The ending

The final paragraph of your text is as important as the first. You need the reader to leave your story with a lasting impression – especially if that reader is an examiner! Always leave yourself plenty of time to think of a good ending. Check out the endings of stories you like reading. They will give you lots of ideas.

1   **Which of the final paragraphs below do you like? Can you say why?**

'I still don't know how Mrs Papa found us. If she wasn't my maths teacher, I would swear she used magic. But then she always was a bit of a witch!'

As he walked back with her, they talked of his plans for the farm. They spoke very little of their feelings for each other. Their shared interests and long friendly relationship had given them a complete understanding of each other's character. This developed after their wedding, into a love that nothing could destroy.

In the summer of this year, we made a journey to Transylvania, and went over the old ground which was, and is, to us so full of vivid and terrible memories. It was almost impossible to believe that the things which we had seen with our own eyes and heard with our own ears were living truths. The castle stood as before, high above a waste of desolation. Castle Dracula.

2   **Now think of a good way to finish your picture story above.**

Written tasks

1   **Your teacher has organised a writing competition based on the pictures you saw earlier. The prize will be announced later! Write the story.**

2   **Write a story for your class magazine which ends with the words: *'Now I think it's time we called the police,' he said.* Look at the USEFUL TIPS below before you begin.**

3   **A BBC magazine is running a series of stories for young people, all ending with the words: *'I haven't stopped laughing yet'*. If your story is good enough, they will publish it in the next edition! Write the story. Look at the USEFUL TIPS below before you begin.**

> **USEFUL TIPS**
> PARAGRAPHS
> Remember to start a new paragraph for each fresh topic. Write a key sentence for each paragraph. Do not write paragraphs consisting of only one line.
> TENSES
> Use the Past Perfect and Past Continuous to set the scene. Use the Simple Past to list dramatic events.
> PLANNING
> Always make a plan before you start. Your story will be clearer, and you will know where to start a new paragraph.

UNIT 8

Writing a balanced report

1 Before you read the report, discuss these questions with a partner.

1 Have you ever been away on a study/business trip? If so, where to?
2 Imagine you could go abroad for a month on a study trip. Where would you like to go and what would you like to study?
3 What would you like to know about the school/the area *before* you left your country? Make a list of the topics: e.g. Travel, Accommodation, Cost.

2 An agency which advertises holiday language courses sent a representative to investigate new schools in England. They asked her to write a report on each school, including negative points, if there were any. This is the report she sent back on one school. Write in the correct heading for each section.

REPORT

To: Ms K Lett
From: Anna Santini
Subject: Brightsea Beach Language School

We visited Brightsea Beach at the end of our trip to England (August 4-12,) and were very impressed by the school and by the environment.

_____: *This* is made up of four separate houses, linked by beautiful gardens. Although classrooms are quite small, they are light and airy. There is a fully-equipped computer centre in the main building, and a well-stocked library.

_____: *Those* we met seemed very friendly and efficient. *All* are well-qualified, and examination results are excellent. We were a little surprised, however, that there were no male teachers apart from the director.

_____: Students stay with host families, carefully selected by the school. *They* provide full board, and will even do washing and ironing.

_____: The school arranges an amazing range of excursions and sports and there is plenty for students to do during the day. However, there is an extra charge for some trips, which might put them beyond the means of some of our students.

_____: *This* is a busy little seaside resort, but, according to the local tourist board office, never unpleasantly crowded. It is also great fun in the evenings.

_____: Prices are quite reasonable compared to the other schools we have seen, apart from the extras mentioned above.

_____: There is no airport near Brightsea and the nearest motorway gets very busy in summer. Travel time to the school could therefore take anything up to four hours.

_____: *This* school would be an ideal place for a holiday course, and the price overall is very competitive. However, we need to look into the problem of transport before we make any final decision.

Activities

Staff

Conclusion

The school

Cost

Potential problems

Accommodation

The environment

3 Now answer the following questions.

1 Notice that the writer has started a new section for each of the topics she wants to write about. Has she included the topics *you* noted down? If not, how would you include your ideas? Would you need more/different headings? What are they? How does she make it clear where each section begins? How does she show clearly what each section will be about?

2 Who wrote the report? Why? Who is going to read it? Do you think they will be happy with the style, content and language of the report? Why?/Why not?

3 Why do you think the writer divided the report into sections, rather than writing just one long text?

4 Which tense is used in most of the text? Why?

The language of reports

Do you think a report like the one you have just seen would *normally* be written in formal or informal style? Why? Which of the phrases below might you expect to find in a report?

1 The service is of an excellent quality.
2 I couldn't stand the waiter!
3 One small disadvantage was the noise from the street.
4 Honestly, I couldn't sleep a wink.
5 Guess what? There's a great big swimming pool.
6 The hotel is so boring.
7 The reception staff were extremely helpful.
8 The beach was so crowded that there wasn't room to swing a cat.
9 I can't think of anything else so I'll end my report here.
10 I have no hesitation in recommending this hotel.

Planning

Complete this spidergraph plan, which Anna made before she wrote the report.

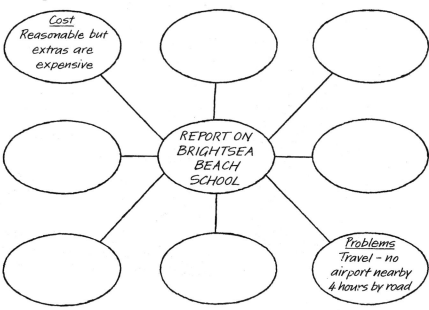

Connecting your text

Your report will be easier to read if you connect the text together.

1 Look at the model again and study the words in italics. Each refers back to another word, earlier in the section. What is it?

2 Choose the most suitable word to connect the following sentences.

1 The hotel is quite expensive. It is ***so*** beyond the reach of many of our customers.
           therefore
           because

2 This resort is well worth a visit. ***Although*** the beach is rocky, it is stunningly beautiful.
           However
           In spite of

3 The night life is exciting. ***However*** the resort is perhaps a little too noisy for families with small children.
           Although
           In spite of

4 The service in the restaurant was not up to standard. ***Although*** the food itself was superb.
           Nevertheless
           Despite

5 ***When*** the beaches are pebbly, they are very quiet and unpolluted.
           While
           As

6 ***Beside*** the noise, I was also annoyed by the lack of attention from the staff.
           Apart from
           Without

7 There were some problems ***nevertheless*** on balance I would thoroughly recommend the hotel.
           but
           however

Redrafting

A business manager has received a leaflet about a country club, which has just opened nearby. If suitable, it will be a good place to take visiting clients. She has asked her new secretary to visit the club and write a report. This is his first draft. He has forgotten how to lay out a report correctly and has also made a number of errors, for example, wrong words, wrong forms and missing words.

Correct the errors (one in each line), and rewrite the text as a report.

Report on Hot Dollar Country Club

Dear Mrs Money,
I visit the Hot Dollar country club last night and was quite
impressed for what I saw, although with certain reservations.
The building. This is large country house with tasteful
decorations and fittings. Downstairs, it is a large lounge
with an open log fire a bar, restaurant and disco. Upstairs,
there is bedrooms and a well-stocked library. *The restaurant*.
The food is of a high standard also prices are very high. The
choice in vegetarian dishes is rather limited. *The bar and disco*.
Excellent. The music in the disco is varied up-to-date. As
for the bar staffs, they are patient and efficient. *The gardens*.
I found the lawns and gardens beautiful. Some of the path are
rather steep, however, especially older club members.
Conclusion. All together, I was impressed for the club. I feel
it is a suitable place entertain our clients and definitely
recommend it. However I think we should speak to owner on the
subject of vegetarian meal and better paths for older members.

Written tasks

1 A new leisure centre has been built in your town/city. You have been asked to visit it and write a balanced report for your employer. The complex, which is a large glass and concrete building, contains: a swimming pool, football and basketball pitches, a fitness suite, a restaurant, a disco, and a cinema.
Group your ideas into sections, with a heading for each section as in the model. Describe the building, its location and the facilities and give your impressions, positive or negative, as appropriate.

2 A tour company are looking for new places to take tourists and are considering an area near you. They are paying you to write a formal, balanced report, giving your opinion on the suitability of the area for tourism. You may like to use the following headings in your report, or you may choose your own.

Places to stay   Places to visit   Other amenities   Nightlife Recommendations

3 You work for a travel company and have been asked to inspect this new, luxury hotel. Write your report.

1. luxurious

2. excellent

3. disappointing

4. excellent

5. beautiful

USEFUL TIPS

LAYOUT
Remember to set out your report clearly, grouping your ideas into sections according to topic. Use headings, clearly underlined.

WRITING A BALANCED REPORT
Remember that in a balanced report you should include negative points if applicable. Try to use the words you practised in this Unit which contrast positive and negative points.

STYLE/REGISTER
In this Unit you are writing formal reports. Make sure your language is polite and formal too.

TENSES
The Present Simple is normally used in this type of report.

UNIT 9

For and against

1 Before you read the text, think about the following questions.

1 Where did you grow up – in a village, in a town, in a city? Do you live in the same place now?
2 Where would you prefer to live – in the city or the countryside? Why?
3 With a partner, think of as many points as you can for and against living in a city.

2 Now read the text below and see how many of the points you thought of are mentioned. Then answer the following questions.

Living in the City–
The High Life or A Nightmare?

SANDRA WILLIAMS OUTLINES THE ADVANTAGES AND DISADVANTAGES OF LIVING IN A CITY

I spent my childhood dreaming of the time when I could leave home and escape to the city. We lived on a farm and, in the winter especially, we were quite cut off from the outside world.

As soon as I left school, I packed my bags and moved to the capital. However I soon discovered that city life has its problems too.

One of the biggest drawbacks is money – it costs so much to go out, not to mention basics like food and rent. Another disadvantage is pollution. I suffer from asthma, and at times the smog is so bad I am afraid to go outside. Then there is the problem of travelling round. Although I have a car, I rarely use it because of the jams. One alternative is to go by bicycle, but that can be quite dangerous.

Of course there are advantages. In the first place, there is so much to do in the city, whatever your tastes in culture or entertainment. In addition, there are wonderful job opportunities, and chances of promotion are greater, too. Finally, if you like shopping, the range of goods is amazing – and, what is more, shops are often only a short walk away.

Is life better then, in the city? Perhaps it is, when you are in your teens or twenties. However, as you get older, and especially if you have small children, the peace of the countryside may seem preferable. I certainly hope to move back there soon.

1 Scan the text again. Where do you think it comes from – a letter, a report, a magazine, a newspaper? Why?
2 What is the writer trying to do – inform, entertain, complain, persuade, give facts? Is the format and language of the text appropriate for this? Why?/Why not?
3 Does the writer give an equal balance of points for and against the topic?
4 There are four paragraphs in the text. What is the topic of each of the paragraphs?

Notes
When writing about the advantages and disadvantages of a topic, it is extremely important to make a clear plan before you begin. Note down points for and against the subject as you think of them; then put the points in order. Try to think of a range of points *on each side* of the argument.

Linking your sentences

In a paragraph, we use words or phrases like these to list fresh points in an argument.

In the first place, ...	In addition, ...	Finally, ...
To begin with, ...	What is more, ...	Last but not least, ...
	Furthermore, ...	
	Then, there is ...	

1 Underline examples in the text you have just read and notice how they are used. Can you add any more to the list?

2 Look at the paragraph below. Some sentences list fresh points in the argument, some develop the point just made. Underline those that list fresh points.

3 Now write out the paragraph again, using the words above, where appropriate, to link the ideas together.

Reasons for not owning a television
There are various reasons why I have never wanted a television. A television is antisocial. Some families I know never speak to each other because they are too engrossed in one programme or another. It is a terrible time waster. You can do so much more if you are not imprisoned in an armchair in front of that little screen. If you do not limit the amount of television your children watch, it can ruin their education. How many kids do their homework well if the TV is always on?

Contrasting

1 **Look at the box below. Notice how we use the words in italics to contrast points in an argument. Do you know any more?**

Although ... *In spite of the fact that ...* *While*	life in the countryside is very peaceful, it can also be lonely.
Life in the countryside is peaceful.	*However, ...* *Nevertheless, ...* *On the other hand ...* it can also be lonely. *In spite of this,*

2 **Now complete these sentences.**

1 Keeping animals in zoos can be cruel. In spite of this, ...
2 If you have a car you can get around easily. On the other hand, ...
3 Although learning a foreign language is hard work, ...
4 Sunbathing can be bad for you. It is, nevertheless, ...
5 While camping holidays can be great fun, ...

Paragraphing

Remember that a paragraph normally consists of a number of sentences grouped round one topic or one aspect of your argument. You start a paragraph on a new line, a little way in from the margin.

The sentences below should form two separate paragraphs but they are jumbled. In pairs, decide which points should be grouped together and in which order. Then, write out the two separate paragraphs. The first sentence of each paragraph is in italics.

- What is more, television can have a serious educational side and there are plenty of good current affairs programmes and documentaries which are very informative.

- While it is good to have such cheap and convenient entertainment in your own living room, it may also mean the end of reading and conversation for large parts of the evening.

- Furthermore, although there are many good programmes on television, there is often far too much blood and violence on the screen.

- *One of the most obvious advantages of having a television is that it offers cheap and convenient entertainment which nearly everyone can afford.*

- This can be especially harmful for children, who will often sit up late at night watching horror films and then have nightmares for days afterwards.

- *On the other hand, having a television can have certain disadvantages.*

- This is especially important for people who are alone all day, or for large families who can't afford to go out to cinemas and theatres.

Planning what to write

1 Work in groups, A and B.

   Group A: Think of as many points as you can *for* each of these topics.

   Group B: Think of as many points as you can *against* each of these topics.

   Getting married

   Keeping animals in zoos

   Owning a car

2 Compare your ideas with other members of the class.

3 Make a list of all the points you have heard *for* and *against* each of the topics. Try to get an equal balance of each.

For	Against
....	....
....	....
....	....
....	....
....	....
....	....
....	....
....	....

Written tasks

1 You have to write a *'For and Against'* article for an English language magazine. Choose one of the topics you discussed in the last exercise and plan your paragraphs. Check your plan with your teacher if possible. Then, write your article.

2 Write an article for your class magazine outlining the advantages and disadvantages of keeping animals in zoos. First, make a list of points before and against, as you did in the last exercise. Remember to plan your introduction and conclusion, too.

USEFUL TIPS

ANSWERING THE QUESTION

Do not confuse a 'For and Against' question with a question which asks for your opinion only, e.g. 'Do you agree with smoking?'. If you are asked to outline the arguments for **and** against a particular topic you must try to be fair and to balance the advantages and disadvantages.

PLANNING

It is absolutely essential to make a plan before you begin this sort of composition. Brainstorm points for and against in two lists, and remember that you should give *both* sides of the argument in full.

PARAGRAPHING

Remember to start a new paragraph each time you change topic.

LINKING SENTENCES

Use the phrases you practised in this Unit to link your sentences together.

UNIT 10 — A formal job application

1 Before you read the job advertisement, think about the following questions.

If you are still a student.
1 What job would you like to do in the future?
2 Do you think you have the right personal qualities and skills for the job?
3 Which of the items in the lists below would be most important in your job?

If you have a job now.
1 What job do you do?
2 Why did you choose it?
3 What sort of personal qualities and skills do you need for your job? (Some of the words below may help you.)

1	2	3	4
patience	humour	good manners	good communication skillls
honesty	ambition	leadership qualities	
intelligence	initiative		
independence	stamina	a sympathetic manner	a sense of humour
reliability	enthusiasm		
efficiency	energy	ability to work under pressure	ability to cope in a crisis
confidence	imagination		
	creativity		

2 Now make adjectives where possible from the nouns in lists 1 and 2.

3 Look at these job advertisements. Which job would you prefer? Why?

TOURIST GUIDE

Do you want to work for one of the most up and coming companies in International Tourism? Do you:

- know this area well?
- have experience in dealing with groups?
- speak at least two languages?

We have a vacancy for a Tourist Guide.

You will need patience, good humour and excellent communication skills. A smart appearance is essential.

Excellent prospects and salary.

Apply in writing to:

Personnel Manager, Eurotours, Granada, Spain.

Trainee Sales Manager Required

A confident, enthusiastic young person is required to train as a Sales Manager in our foreign book sales department. You will need excellent communication skills, plus a good command of English. A smart appearance and pleasant manner are essential. Prospects are excellent for applicants who can take responsibility and who really want to get to the top.

Apply in writing to:
Shortman Publishing House
9, Clifton Street
Kensington,
London WC6 8LP

WORK FOR NTV RADIO!

New world service radio station is looking for

talented young people

for a variety of opportunities, both as presenters and behind the scenes.

- Applicants must be imaginative, reliable and self-confident.
- Training will be given where required but a high degree of hard work and commitment will be demanded in return.
- Ability to keep cool in a crisis essential!
- Applicants must speak good English.

Salary negotiable, depending on experience.

Apply, in writing, to:
NTV Radio, PO Box 892, London W1

4 What are all the qualities you think you would need for each of the jobs? Make some notes under these headings:

Tourist Guide   Sales Manager   Radio Presenter

5 Look at the Tourist Guide advertisement. Underline the most important details which you should refer to in a letter of application.

6 Now imagine you are the Personnel Manager of Eurotours. What sort of person are you looking for? What do you need to hear from a good applicant? How formal would you expect their letter to be?

Pairwork

Student A: Imagine you are going to interview someone for a job like the one in the first advertisement (Tourist Guide). Use the ideas in the box to write some questions. When your partner is ready, begin the interview.

Student B: Imagine you are applying for a job like the one in the first advertisement. Note down some (imaginary) details about yourself. Use the questions in the box to help you. When you are ready, begin the interview.

EXPERIENCE
Have you ever .....?
How long have you .....?

When did you .....?
In your last job, did you .....?

LANGUAGES
How many .....?
How well .....? ..... certificates?
..... ever lived abroad?

KNOWLEDGE OF AREA
How well .....?
What do you think a group of ..... people might like to visit?

PERSONAL QUALITIES
How ..... with customers who complain about everything?
What ...... your best qualities?

HOBBIES
What .....?
..... belong to any clubs?

WHAT IF?
What would you do if .....?

WHY?
Why do you think we ..... you the job?

A letter of application

This is the letter one of the applicants wrote for the job of Tourist Guide.

1 Do you think Eurotours will be impressed by his/her letter? Has he/she supplied all the details requested? Is the language and style he/she uses formal or informal? Is this appropriate? Has he/she included any unnecessary information?

2 The words in bold type are important because they help to link the text together. They refer back to words or information given earlier in the text. Mark the words they refer to, as shown in the example.

4 Green Street
Kensington
London

5 August, 199–

Personnel Manager
Eurotours
Calle Principal
Granada
Spain

Dear Sir/Madam,

I saw your advertisement for a (Tourist Guide) in this week's edition of 'Travel' and would like to apply for the post.

As my c.v. shows, I am very well qualified for (this job.) I studied Tourism at London University from 1992-5 and obtained the enclosed Diploma. As you can see, **this** included a special course on tourism in Europe. Since leaving University, I have also done a number of training courses in different aspects of the tourist industry (certificates enclosed).

For the past year, I have been working as a courier here in England. In **this job**, my main responsibilities include guiding groups around the city and dealing with bookings and accommodation.

Before **that**, I had a job with Smith's Travel Agency in London. **There**, I answered telephone enquiries and dealt with holiday bookings.

My mother is Spanish and I therefore have a perfect understanding of Spanish people, their language and the country. I know Andalucia especially well as I have spent most of my holidays around **this region**.

As regards languages, I speak Spanish and French fluently. In addition to **these**, I am at present taking classes in German.

I would now like to broaden my experience as a courier. I would also welcome the chance to work for a large company like yours, with the chances for promotion **this** would provide.

In my spare time I play basketball for a local team **of which** I have recently been made captain. I also help out with the local youth club.

As you can see from my references, I have plenty of patience and good humour. In fact I have been named 'Courier Of The Month' by our local tourist board on two occasions.

I would be able to come for interview at any time.
I look forward to hearing from you.

Yours faithfully,

Chris Jones

Chris Jones

Verbs and prepositions

Complete the sentences with an appropriate preposition and the correct form of the verb (gerund or infinitive).

1 I am interested ..... (*apply*) for the post.
2 I would like the chance ..... (*widen*) my experience.
3 I am looking forward ..... (*meet*) my colleagues.
4 I have got a lot of experience ..... (*deal*) with groups.
5 This job would give me the opportunity ..... (*travel*).
6 I hope ..... (*hear*) from you soon.

Written tasks

1 Study this spidergraph. It is the plan the candidate made before he/she wrote the letter of application you saw earlier.

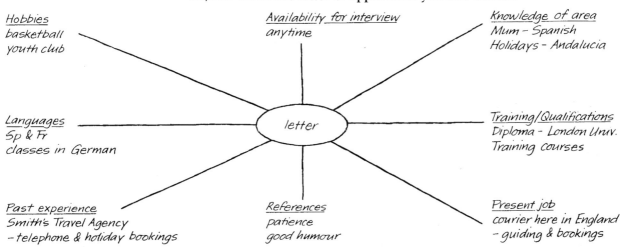

Hobbies
basketball
youth club

Availability for interview
anytime

Knowledge of area
Mum – Spanish
Holidays – Andalucia

Languages
Sp & Fr
classes in German

letter

Training/Qualifications
Diploma – London Univ.
Training courses

Past experience
Smith's Travel Agency
– telephone & holiday bookings

References
patience
good humour

Present job
courier here in England
– guiding & bookings

2 Write a letter of application for one of the jobs advertised at the beginning of this Unit.

USEFUL TIPS

STYLE/REGISTER
Remember to use very polite, formal language for letters of application.

TENSES
The Present Perfect Simple and Continuous are useful if you are talking about recent work and experience.

LINKING YOUR TEXT TOGETHER
Check back to the exercise on text linking that you did in this Unit. Try to do the same with your text.

DRAFTING
Nobody writes a perfect text the first time. There are always words that need changing or errors to correct. After you have written a first draft of your letter, exchange your work with your partner. Check each other's work for errors in spelling, punctuation and paragraphing. Then rewrite the text with any other changes you need to make.

UNIT 11

Giving opinions

1 Before you read the article, think about the following questions.

1 Nowadays, scientists can do things which our grandparents would never have believed possible Can you think of examples?
2 How much do you know about genetic engineering?
  – What are genes? What do they control?
  – How can scientists use genetics in
  a) medicine?
  b) farming?
  Do you think this is always a good thing?

Scientists breed first fruit fly with eyes on its legs and wings

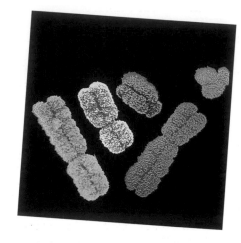

Man Given Pig Heart

2 Read this article about genetic engineering. Do you agree with the writer? Why?/Why not?

talking point

This week's topic: GENETIC SCIENCE

Scientists have made amazing discoveries over the last twenty years, especially in the field of genetics. Already they can create strange new species of plants and animals. They may soon be able to design new kinds of human beings. Do scientists really know what they are doing, and should we let them go on?

I think genetic engineering should be very carefully controlled. To begin with, life on our planet has evolved slowly, over thousands of years. If we change that process too quickly by tampering with genes, which are the building blocks of nature, we may cause terrible damage. I worry, furthermore, where scientists will stop if we allow them to 'play God' with our world, and whether they will be able to control the changes they are unleashing. Lastly, we should consider how some governments could use genetics. They might try to create 'the perfect baby' or design a 'master-race'. This is a nightmare scenario, of course, but it could happen.

It is true that genetic engineering can be used for the good, to detect or even cure disease. Biotechnology can be commercially profitable, too, in farming and in agriculture. To my mind, however, these factors still do not outweigh the dangers.

In the wrong hands, genetic engineering can be used as a way of playing with nature. Nobody knows what the effects will be if we allow this to go on without strict controls. I think all of us should stop and think before we allow scientists to develop these techniques any further – our survival could depend on it!

TV star Pat Kennedy gives her opinion.

3 Now answer the following questions.

1 Underline the topic sentence in each paragraph.
2 Which paragraph in the model:
   – gives the writer's opinion and reasons for it?
   – restates the problem and the writer's opinion?
   – sets out the problem in general and states why it is controversial?
   – gives the other side of the argument and the reasons why the writer isn't convinced by them?

4 Read the article below, which gives a different opinion. It is only in draft form, and there are grammatical errors. Can you correct them?

Pop star Don Jackson gives his view.

Some of the most exciting progress in the science has happen in the field of genetics. It is now possible to grow plants who do not get diseases, and to breed cows which produce more milk. The scientists can even create new types of animals.

In my opinion, these development are very good news. In the first place, doctors will soon be able to use the genetic engineering to help fighting disease. They can tell you if there is a medical problem in your family which it could be passed on to your children. Hopefully, he may then be able to alter the genes and cure disease. Secondly, genetics are important in agriculture. Scientists can now create the plants which are resistant to disease. This is particularly important on poor countries where people starve if the harvest will be bad. Finally, farmers can breed animals who produce more food, and are therefore more profitably.

People sometimes argues that genetic engineering should be stop. They think scientific advance is 'unnatural'. However, I believe that scientists and doctors can trusted to use this knowledge responsibly. After all, peoples protested about things like transplant surgery at the past but most people are in favour now. I feel sure that, in the future, genetic engineering is of enormous benefit to us of all.

(Margin markings left: A, WW, A, A, G, G, G, WW, G, G, G, G)
(Margin markings right: G, G, G, G, G, G, G, WW)

5 Discuss the following questions with a partner.

Does each writer put forward a logical argument for his/her opinion? What is it? Which opinion do you agree with most?

Speaking and writing about opinions

1 Study the language we use when speaking about opinions. Can you add any more phrases?

Well, I think that …
To my mind …
If you ask me, …
Surely you agree that …

That's right! And don't you think that …
I quite agree! I think …

That's rubbish! I think …
Really? I'm afraid I don't agree. To my mind …

2 Now discuss the topics below with a partner.

Should smoking be made illegal?
Should we all be vegetarians?
Should we execute criminals?

Make a note of some of the ideas that came up during your discussion. You will need them later.

3 These phrases can be used to write about opinions. Can you add any more?

AGREEING	DISAGREEING
In my opinion,	I do not agree that ...
I think	I do not think that ...
I believe	
As I see it,	
I tend to think	I tend to disagree with the idea that ...

4 Now, write one sentence on each of the topics you have just discussed, stating your opinion and the reason for it, e.g. 'As I see it, the only way to stop people from smoking and reduce the incidence of cancer and heart disease is by making cigarettes illegal.'

Sequencing words

1 Look back to the model articles in this Unit and underline the words the writers use to list arguments, e.g. *To begin with* ..., and *Finally*, ...

2 Can you add any more words or phrases to this list of sequencing words?

First of all, ...	Moreover, ...	Lastly, ...
In the first place, ...	In addition ...	Last but not least ...

3 A writer made these notes for an article called 'Wives who work'. Sort the notes into the best order and write *one* paragraph, using sequencers where appropriate.

> I believe everyone should be free to choose the sort of life that will make them happy, without being made to feel guilty.
>
> We should not forget that men should be equally involved in caring for their children and that one solution could be for them to stay at home and be a 'house-husband'.
>
> I think married women with young children should definitely go out to work if that is what they want.
>
> There is no reason why companies can't provide crèches for those women who do make this choice. Young children can then be well looked after during working hours.

4 Use your own ideas to write a similar paragraph on *one* of the following questions:

Should smoking be made illegal? *Should we all be vegetarians?*

Putting the other side

1 Work with a partner. Imagine you are at a government meeting called to discuss the idea: *'Should girls and boys be educated separately?'*

Person A: You have a teenage daughter. You agree with this idea. Tell your neighbour what you think.
Person B: You have a teenage son. You do not agree with this idea. Tell your neighbour what you think.

When writing your side of an argument, it is a good idea to mention the other side of the case and then show why you do not agree.

2   Write a short paragraph on the topic you have just discussed, setting out one or two of the arguments used against you and saying why you do not agree with them.

Written tasks

1   You have been asked to write an article in English for your school magazine on whether boys and girls should be educated separately. You may like to use the plan below as a guide. You should use at least two separate paragraphs for the Development section.

Introduction   What is the situation at the moment in your school/country? Is this a satisfactory situation?

Development   1 Give your opinion and list the reasons for it.
                 2 Mention the other side of the argument briefly and say why you disagree.

Conclusion   Summarise your arguments and restate your opinion clearly.

2   Write an article for an English-speaking magazine giving your opinion on one of the topics you have discussed in this Unit. Remember to make a plan before you start.

3   Write an article for your school magazine entitled: *'Will life in the future be better than now?'*

Think about:
– pollution and nature   – computers and automation
– scientific discoveries   – population
– medical progress
Remember to make a plan before you start.

Reviews and reports on set books

1 Before you read the report, think about the following questions.

1 How many different categories of book can you think of, e.g. romance, adventure, thriller? Which is your favourite category?

2 Look at each of the book covers. What does it suggest to you about the book itself? What category of book do you think it is? What is it probably about? Would the cover make *you* want to read the book? Why?/Why not?

3 In your opinion, which is the best book ever written? Which is *your* favourite? Why?

2 Read this review that a librarian has written for a school book display.

BOOK REVIEW

TITLE: Frankenstein

AUTHOR: Mary Shelley

CATEGORY: Classic, horror

PLOT:

This story is set in Switzerland, many years ago. Victor Frankenstein is a passionate young man who is fascinated by science, and by the forces of nature he sees at work in the mountains and lakes around him.

When he is old enough, he goes to University to study science. At first his studies go well, but he soon becomes obsessed by a mysterious and forbidden type of investigation - how to create life itself.

When Victor's friend Henri comes to stay, he makes a gruesome find. Victor has a 'laboratory' in his flat, with jars full of human limbs. Even worse, in the middle of the room there is a bath - and in the bath lies the body of a man!

Henri realises that Victor is planning to bring the man to life. The experiment succeeds, but the body is scarred and deformed in the process and Frankenstein is horrified by the 'monster' he has created. The man escapes - and the horror begins!

COMMENTS:

This is an exciting novel. Although written long ago, it is still a tale to send shivers down your spine! Most readers will find it hard to put down.

3 Divide these words into the three lists below.

producer, publisher, author, reader, chapter, scene, plot, character, actor, audience, hero, paperback, box-office hit, classic, best-seller

Books	Films	Both
....	....	....
....	....	....
....	....	....

4 Scan the text again. Who is writing? For what purpose? Who is going to read the report? Why has the writer divided his/her text into sections? Is the format and language appropriate for the readers he/she has in mind? Why?/Why not?

5 Now answer the following questions.

1 Look at the PLOT section of the review. What information are we given in each of the paragraphs? Complete the paragraph plan below.

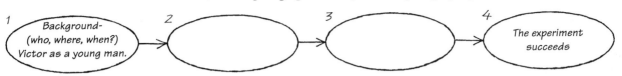

1 Background– (who, where, when?) Victor as a young man. → 2 → 3 → 4 The experiment succeeds

2 What tenses are used to tell the story? Give examples.
3 What information are we given in the COMMENTS section?
4 Look at the book cover. How does it relate to the book? Does it illustrate a crucial event in the story/depict a character who is essential to the plot? Does it make the book look interesting to someone who hasn't read it? Why/Why not?
5 *Frankenstein* is the story of a scientist who wants to 'play God'. Is this theme relevant to us nowadays?

Vocabulary

Complete the sentences with an appropriate word.

1 The first three ..... of the book were very exciting.
2 ..... of science fiction will love this novel.
3 This is the first novel I have read by this ..... .
4 James Bond is one of the best known ..... in spy fiction.
5 The story is ..... in South America.
6 Hardback novels are usually more expensive than ..... .
7 The ..... of the novel is a country girl called Tess.
8 The ..... was quite complicated and difficult to follow.

Relative pronouns

1 Compare the two plot summaries below. Which is the best? Why?

A The hero, Victor, is a young man. Victor creates a monster. It runs away into the forest.

B The hero, Victor, is a young man **who becomes obsessed by the idea that he can create life**. Victor creates a monster **which is so scarred and deformed that he can't bear to look at it.** It runs away into the forest, **where it lives on berries and on water from the river.**

When you describe the plot of a book, try to write more than just a list of events. Giving extra details will make your text more interesting.

2 Here is the skeleton of a spy story. Expand the story, using the information below. Use relative pronouns where appropriate.

> The film is about a secret agent called James Clark. An important mission takes him to Switzerland. He has a number of secret weapons, including a car and a watch. While he is having dinner at the hotel, he meets a young woman. She is desperately trying to hide from a man with a scar. Later, she and James take a crowded cable car to the top of a nearby mountain.
>
> They spend some hours in a bar, in romantic mood. On their way back down the mountain, the cable car comes to a sudden stop. For a moment there is silence. Then they hear the sound of a helicopter. The pilot has a gun trained on the cable car!

He works for British Intelligence.
He has been specially chosen for the mission by 'Control'.
It can go underwater.
It shoots poisoned darts.
He is based at the hotel.
She, of course, is young, cool and very beautiful.
She suspects the man with a scar is trying to kill her.
The cable car is now empty.
It is coming towards them over the mountain peak.
The woman suddenly recognises the pilot as the man with the scar.

Contrasting facts

When you write your comments on a book you may want to make contrasting statements.

1 Study these examples.

> It was written long ago **but** it is still topical.
>
> *Although it was written long ago, it is still topical.*
> *It is still topical, **in spite of the fact that** it was written long ago.*

2 Now join these pairs of sentences in each of the ways shown above.

1 The book is exciting on the whole. Some parts of it tend to drag.
2 I enjoyed the book. I couldn't really recommend it.
3 I had no idea who the murderer was. I got all the clues.
4 The book was 500 pages long. I still enjoyed it.
5 I wasn't impressed by the film. I loved the book.

Discussion

Ask your partner about a book he/she has read recently. Find out:

What type of book it is.
Why he/she chose it.
Where the story is set.
Who the main characters are.
What, briefly, the story is about (what is the plot).
What he/she thought of it.
If he/she would recommend it to the class.

You may find the language in the box helpful.

Written tasks

1 Your teacher has asked you to describe the plot of a set book you are reading. She is hoping that other students in the class will then become interested in reading the book. Use the plot section in the review at the beginning of this Unit as a guide to your writing.

2 You have been asked to write a report on a book you are reading for a class magazine. The review you write will help other students in their choice of reading. You may like to use the plan below as a guide.

Introduction What type of book is it? Where is it set? Who are the main characters?

Development The plot. Describe events in the order in which they happen in the story. Try not to make your account too complicated – pick out a few of the most important events. Remember that the person reading your report cannot ask questions if something is not clear!

Conclusion What did you think of the book? Why? Was it well written/exciting/imaginative? Would you recommend it to others?

3 Describe the front cover of a book you are reading and say if and how it illustrates the story and characters. Does it make the book look interesting enough to read? Your teacher will use what you write for a class book exhibition.

UNIT 13 — Articles for newspapers and magazines

1 Before you read the newspaper article, think about the following questions.

1 Do you read newspapers and magazines? How often? Do you ever read British ones? If so, which? (If possible, bring one to class.)
2 Do you like your newspapers and magazines to a) inform you? b) entertain you?, or c) do a mixture of both?
3 Do you think that the style of a newspaper which reports serious news will be different from a newspaper which wants to entertain? In what way?

2 Read this newspaper article. The headline is a pun (a play on words). Can you explain it?

Thief Comes Unstuck!

Carlos Villa is no stranger to crime. He was first arrested for shoplifting at the age of twelve. Since then, he has regularly appeared in court, charged with pickpocketing, petty theft and burglary. His offences have never made the newspapers, though, until this week.

The story began when Carlos broke into a glue factory, with a view to stealing the petty cash. It was late Saturday evening and all the staff had gone home for the weekend. The factory was in complete darkness and Carlos was groping his way through the building when he noticed an unusual smell. He stopped and inhaled deeply.

Unfortunately for him, the smell was coming from some leaking tins of glue. The fumes were very strong and he fainted. As he collapsed to the floor, he knocked over more tins, – and stuck himself firmly to the ground.

He was found 34 hours later, when the factory opened again after the weekend break. The fire brigade was called and he was eventually freed. He was then taken to the local hospital, where he is now recovering from his ordeal.

'He swears he'll go straight after this,' his girlfriend told me yesterday. Let's hope he sticks to his promise this time!

Note

Writing an article for a newspaper or magazine often requires narrative techniques. Money and space usually limit the length of an article so the writing must be precise, and paragraphs are often very short. The final paragraph often includes comments or quotations from a spokesperson.

3 Now answer the following questions.

1 What information are we given in each paragraph of this article? Complete the boxes.

1 Introduction - Background His past crimes → 2 → 3 → 4 → 5

2 How many different past tense forms can you find in the text? What are they? Which tenses are used to paint the background in paragraph 2?

Narrative tenses

Here is a report about a football match. Underline the correct verbs.

The Cup Final between Atletico and Hellas *has taken / took place* earlier today. Against the odds, Hellas *had won / won* in an exciting finish.

The game *just began / had just begun* when Spiros, one of Hellas's best players, *has been / was* sent off the field for fighting. Atletico *have taken / took* advantage of their position and *have scored / scored* soon afterwards. After that, although Hellas came near to scoring many times, the points *were staying / stayed* the same.

Then, unbelievably, just when everyone *got / was getting* ready to leave, Hellas came back and scored twice. The crowd went crazy!

'That *was / had been* the most exciting final I *have ever watched! / ever watched!*' said team coach Thanasis.

Writing for newspapers and magazines

True or False? Which statements do you agree with?

Articles in magazines and newspapers:
1 never contain phrasal verbs.
2 are often dramatic.
3 are not divided into paragraphs.
4 never include quotes.
5 attract your attention if the headline or first paragraph is original and interesting.
6 can be formal or informal, depending on the type of reader they are written for.

The passive

1 Which of these two sentences would you expect to find in a newspaper? Why? What makes it the most effective?

a) **A SCORPION HAS BEEN DISCOVERED IN A SANDWICH!**

b) **SOMEONE HAS DISCOVERED A SCORPION IN A SANDWICH!**

2 Look back to the report at the beginning of this Unit and underline all the examples of the passive.
Why do you think passives are used so much in newspapers?

3 Look at the following sentences. How do you change a sentence from *active* to *passive*?

ACTIVE	PASSIVE
*Thieves **steal** money.*	→ *Money **is stolen** by thieves.*
*The Queen **will open** the hospital.*	→ *The hospital **will be opened** by the Queen*
*Police **questioned** passers-by.*	→ *Passers-by **were questioned** by police.*
*Someone **has discovered** a new species of animal.*	→ *A new species of animal **has been discovered**.*

4 Complete these rules for changing a sentence from *active* to *passive*.

1 Make the *object* of the active sentence into the ..... of the passive sentence.
2 Use the verb 'to .....' in the same tense as the main verb.
3 Add the ..... Participle of the main verb.

5 Now change these sentences in the same way.

1 Someone has won £10,000 in the lottery.
2 They are questioning the lucky winner at the moment.
3 They have interviewed the man on television.
4 They are going to keep his name secret.

Vocabulary

Newspaper reports often deal with accidents and crimes.

1 Complete this list of crime-related words.

Verb	Person	Crime
to steal	thief	theft
....	robber	....
....	....	burglary
to blackmail	....	....
....	kidnapper	....
....	....	hijacking
....	....	mugging
to murder	....	....
to joyride	....	....

2 Now match the two parts of the sentences below.

1 She witnessed   a insurance
2 There was an accident, but nobody was   b the flat
3 Police interviewed   c clues
4 The car was badly   d injured
5 Thieves broke into   e the victim
6 The police found fingerprints but no other   f an accident
7 He recovered his money from his   g damaged

First and final paragraphs

The first and final paragraphs of a news story are very important. If the first paragraph is not interesting, the reader may well not bother to read the story at all – or may not even buy the newspaper!

In the news article on page 63, the first and final paragraphs are missing. Think about the questions below, then complete the article.

First paragraph	Final paragraph
How many fans were injured?	Has a spokesperson for the club made any comment?
Where was the match?	Any quotes from family or friends?
When was it?	Have any lessons been learnt for future matches?
Which teams were playing?	

TWENTY INJURED AT FOOTBALL MATCH

-- .

The accident happened when United scored their first gaol. As fans surged forward, a barrier collapsed and people were trapped and trampled underfoot. A fleet of ambulances took the injured to a local hospital, and twenty people have been detained. Two of these are in a critical condition.

----------------------------------- .

Written tasks

1 Thieves broke into a house in your neighbourhood a few days ago. Write an article for your class newspaper. The questions below may give you some ideas. Make a plan and number the items before you start to write. Give your article a suitable headline!

- Where did this happen? To whom? When? What was stolen?
- How did the thieves get in? What did they do? Where were the usual occupants? Was anyone hurt?
- Did anyone see the thieves? Have the police got any clues?
- How likely is it that the police will catch the thieves? Any quotes from police, victims or neighbours?

Get your partner to check your first draft for errors in punctuation, spelling and paragraphing. Then write a second draft to show your teacher.

2 Write an article for your school newspaper about a car crash you witnessed. Remember to make a plan before you start.

USEFUL TIPS

STYLE

Before you write, remember to consider *who* is going to read your article and *why*. If you think your readers want drama, use dramatic language! If you think they are very serious readers, make your style more formal and factual.

PARAGRAPHING

Remember to start a new paragraph for each section of the article.

TENSES

The Past Continuous and Past Perfect tenses are used to paint the background to an action. Remember that the passive is often found in newspapers.

UNIT 14

Describing festivals and ceremonies

1 Before you read the text, answer the following questions.

1 Look at these photographs and say what is happening.

2 Can you describe any special days or festivals celebrated in Great Britain?

2 Now scan the text below. Who is the author? Who is he writing for? What aspects of the festival does he think his readers will want to know about? Does he make the description interesting? Does he use a good range of vocabulary and structure? Give examples to illustrate your point of view.

School Magazine

Notting Hill Carnival

Yiannis, from Class 6, describes a festival he took part in while on holiday in Great Britain.

The most colourful street event in England is the Notting Hill Carnival. It is held in London each August Bank Holiday. The festival celebrates the traditions of the British black community who emigrated to Britain from the West Indies in the 1950s. They brought the Caribbean idea of 'carnival' – with magnificent processions, colourful costumes, steel bands, reggae and street dancing.

Preparations begin weeks beforehand. Costumes and masks are carefully designed and lorries decorated. Steel bands rehearse. Huge loudspeakers are placed in the streets to carry the throbbing beat of reggae over the roar of London traffic. Shortly before the festival, the streets are decorated with dazzling red, green and yellow streamers.

The carnival lasts for three days and is a glorious feast of music and colour. A stunning procession of floats followed by dancers in exotic and original costumes parades through the narrow London streets. There are street entertainers of all kinds and stalls sell thirst-quenching tropical fruits, such as fresh pineapple, water melons and mangoes. Thousands of people watch the carnival, and everybody sways and dances, black and white, young and old! Even the policemen on duty take part in the fun. For these three carefree days in August, a little Caribbean magic touches the grey streets of London.

3 **Answer the following questions.**

1 Each paragraph in the article describes a different aspect of the festival. What information are we given in each paragraph?
2 The passive is often used when describing festivals, carnivals and other such events. Find examples of this in the article.
3 Carnivals and festivals are usually regular annual events. What verb tenses should be used to describe such events?

Vocabulary

To make a description come alive, you need to use a range of adjectives and adverbs.

1 **Look back to the text and underline the adjectives and adverbs.**

2 **Make adjectives from the nouns below, then put them in the appropriate column, according to the ending.**

beauty, nation, colour, outrage, tradition, dread, glory, origin, wonder, magic, marvel

graceful	musical	dangerous
beautiful	....	....
....	....	....
....	....	....
....	....	....

Can you add any more examples to each list?

3 **Read this text about a festival in India. Help the writer to make the text more vivid by adding your own choice of adjectives or adverbs. Use the pictures and your imagination to help!**

Diwali, 'The Festival of Lights', is an ..... Indian festival. It is held in October or early November, when the ..... nights remind us winter is approaching. Families decorate the windows and doors of their houses with ..... lamps and the ..... light shines out in the streets. There are ..... fireworks in the evenings and the sky is full of ..... colours. In some parts of India, girls put ..... lamps into the river and leave them to float away. If the light does not go out, it is considered good luck.

Prepositions

Complete the sentences with an appropriate preposition (your dictionary will help!).

1 The streets are brightly decorated ..... streamers.
2 The dancers make their way ..... the London streets.
3 The streets are lined ..... stalls selling tropical fruits.
4 The procession is watched ..... thousands of people.
5 Many West Indians came to Britain ..... the 1950s.
6 Thousands of people take part ..... the celebrations.
7 The carnival is held ..... August.
8 The dancers are dressed ..... exotic costumes.
9 The instruments are made ..... old oil drums.
10 It is the largest street event ..... Europe.

Passives

1 **When we are describing a festival, we often use the passive. Look back to the text. Can you say *why* the passive is used?**

2 **Look at these examples. Do you remember how to form the passive? Complete the rules.**

1 Change the object to ..... .
2 Use the verb 'to .....' in the same tense as the original.
3 Put the Past ..... of the main verb.

ACTIVE		PASSIVE
They **have to** design costumes.	$\rightarrow$	Costumes **have to be** designed.
They **decorate** streets with streamers.	$\rightarrow$	Streets **are** decorated with streamers.

3 **Now change the sentences below in the same way.**

1 People often exchange gifts.
2 They perform traditional dances.
3 They must wear national costume.
4 People usually cook a special meal.
5 People often begin preparations months before.
6 They push the heaviest floats through the streets.
7 They always give the children a holiday.
8 They do not allow traffic to pass.

4 **Discuss these questions with your partner.**

1 What is the most enjoyable festival/carnival you have ever taken part in? Where, when and why is it held?
2 What sort of preparations are made? How long before the festival do they begin?
3 What happens on the day of the festival? Are any special clothes worn? Is any special food cooked?
4 Is anything special arranged for the evening?
5 Are any special activities arranged for the children?
6 Is the festival still very popular nowadays? If not, why?

Making notes

1   Make notes about the festival you have just described to your partner. You may like to use these headings, or invent your own.

Name of Festival: Where, when, why is it celebrated?
Preparations:
Costumes:
Food:
The day's events:
Evening activities:
Events for the children:
Other details:

2   Now decide how you will group this information into paragraphs. Will you use a new paragraph for each heading – or can you group two sections together? In which order will you describe the headings? Number them before you start.

Written tasks

1   An English speaking magazine is running a writing competition. The winning text will be printed in next month's issue. The title is: *'Describe a popular festival/carnival in your country.'* Write your entry, using the plan you made earlier. Add some photographs too, if you can!

2   A group of English-speaking officials are coming to visit your class. Your teacher wants to make a classroom display, with descriptions and photographs of typical events or ceremonies in your country, e.g. weddings, Christmas, etc. Write an article for the display. Supply some photographs too, if you can!

USEFUL TIPS

ADJECTIVES/ADVERBS
Use a good range of these to make your description more vivid.
PLANNING
You may like to use the headings you saw earlier in this Unit to plan your work.
TENSES
You will need the Present Simple to describe activities. Remember that the passive is often used to describe preparations and celebrations, too.

UNIT 15

Describing a fictional character

1 **Before you read the letter, think about the following questions.**

1 Who is your favourite character in a) fiction and b) the cinema? Why? Describe him/her.
2 Which character from fiction would you most like to spend an evening with? Why?

You know the name   You know the numb[er]

GOLDENEYE

2 **Quickly scan the letter on page 69 in which a famous fictional character describes his first meeting with his partner. Who are the two people?**

3 **Now read the letter again and answer these questions.**

1 Who is writing the letter? To whom? Why?
2 How well do they know each other?
3 What does the writer think his correspondent really wants to know?
4 Does the letter contain appropriate vocabulary for that purpose? Give examples.

London
Friday

My dear friend Henry,

Two months ago, I retired from my post as an army doctor in India due to ill health. When I got back to London I had no friends and nowhere to live. Then one day, quite out of the blue, an acquaintance took me to meet someone who was looking for a fellow lodger. Within a few moments, this stranger had told me my life history. I was fascinated. The very next evening we were sharing rooms at 221B Baker Street.

My new friend's appearance is really striking. He is over six feet tall, and extremely thin. He has sharp, piercing eyes, a thin hawk-like nose and a square, prominent chin. His whole expression is alert and decisive. As for his clothes, he is quite fashionable. He is very fond of tweeds – and he has a 'deerstalker' hat which he wears all the time when we are not in London.

He is extremely polite and considerate to strangers but doesn't seem to need many friends. I'm afraid he is also quite moody at home, and very untidy – but then so am I !

His hobby is playing the violin, which he does especially wildly when the mood takes him! He also smokes a pipe, which I don't like much. He loves doing chemical experiments and spends hours messing about with test tubes and potions.

It seems he is a private detective of some kind, and he has asked me to help him with his next case. I have a feeling it could be quite interesting!

Must rush now

Best wishes
Dr Watson

Planning

1 Complete this plan (*How we met* and *Personality*) which the writer made before he started the letter.

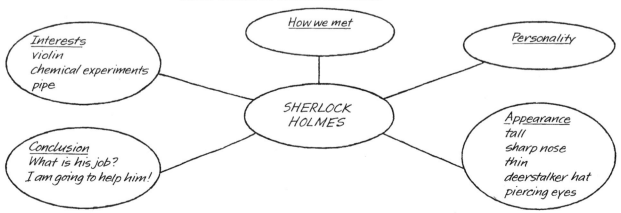

2 The plan helped him to divide his letter into paragraphs. How?

Vocabulary

Imagine you are inventing characters for a Sherlock Holmes story. You need a hero, a heroine and a villain. Make a list of the adjectives you could use to describe the character of each of them.
e.g.

Heroine	Hero	Villain
independent	brave	desperate
passionate	cool	ill-tempered
gentle	patient	rough
....	....	....
....	....	....

Punctuation

Jane Eyre is a classic British novel, written in the nineteenth century. A teacher has asked his/her students to write a character study of their favourite character from the novel. This student has not planned his/her work, and has therefore forgotten all he/she learnt about paragraphs! He/She has also forgotten to proofread the text and has left a lot of punctuation mistakes.

1 **Divide the text into five paragraphs. Then correct the punctuation and capital letters.**

the character I like most is the heroine herself jane Eyre she is the opposite of the helpless limp heroines of many love stories. in fact the spirited way in which she faces disaster makes her in many ways a modern woman. As a child, Jane is already passionately strong-willed. This is partly why she is sent to boarding school where she is treated appallingly but her spirit is never broken. she develops into a calm self-possessed independent young woman After she leaves the school, she finds work as a governess and falls in love with her employer a mysterious, brooding, quick-tempered man called Mr Rochester. Stung by his apparent cruelty she declares her love for him – even though as a woman and a governess this takes great courage even when she discovers that he is already married she does not become self-pitying or bitter With typical courage and determination she sets out to find the right path through disaster Jane Eyre is a brilliant study of a sensitive intelligent and fiercely independent woman I enjoyed reading her story – and I'm sure you will, too!

2 **Now finish the plan the writer should have made before he/she started to write.**

Paragraph 1
The reason I chose Jane. Why she is a 'modern' woman.
Paragraph 2
Paragraph 3
Paragraph 4
Paragraph 5

Extending your vocabulary

Having a wide range of vocabulary is very important if you want to write well, and it is one of the main things examiners look for! You can extend your vocabulary by reading widely, by listening, and by using a good dictionary. Keep a special book to write new words in – and test yourself to see if you can remember them!

These types of exercises will help to increase your vocabulary, too.

1   **Underline all the adjectives in the description of Jane Eyre. Then find a synonym among them for the words in this list.**

weak   self-reliant
fiery   composed
enigmatic   impatient
clever   sulky

2   **Form nouns from these adjectives.**

determined   mysterious   intelligent
independent   bitter   cruel
passionate   courageous   calm
self-pitying   sensitive

Text comparison

The two texts we have seen in this Unit both involve character description but were written for very different purposes and readers. It is very important to remind yourself *before you start writing* both **who** you are writing for and **why**. These two questions will then give you a guide to the format, style and language you should use.

Written tasks

1   **Imagine you recently spent an evening with one of your favourite characters from fiction (book or film). Write a letter to a friend describing how you met the character, and his or her appearance, personality and interests. Do not forget to make a plan before you start. Your teacher may deduct a mark if you forget!**

2   **Write a character study of the person you like most in any book you have studied recently. Your teacher will use your work as part of a classroom display so that parents, teachers and students in other classes can read about the book or film. Your plan will also be on display, so do not forget to make one!**

3   **You have entered a competition and have been asked to invent a character for a new James Bond film. (The prize is a trip to Hollywood!) The description must begin with the words: *'James had just returned from his mission in China when a new character entered his life'*. Make notes under the following headings before you begin:**

    How they met   Appearance   Dress   Personality   Conclusion

USEFUL TIPS

STYLE/REGISTER
Look carefully at the Written task and check who is going to read your text.
Then decide how formal or how friendly your language should be.

VOCABULARY
Try and use some of the adjectives and nouns you learnt in this Unit.

PROOFREADING
Read your work over carefully when you have finished. Reading it aloud to a friend can help to find punctuation errors. Use a dictionary to check any spellings you are not sure of.

UNIT 16

Reports on travel and holidays

1 Before you read the report, think about the following questions.

1 Where did you spend your last holiday?
2 Who did you go with?
3 What sort of holiday was it?

2 Scan the text below and match each section with one of the headings.

3 Where do you think the report comes from? What is the writer's purpose in writing the report – to persuade, to interest, to give an opinion? Is the format appropriate for a holiday report? Why?/Why not?

Lazy days

Those teeth bite!

Beneath the sea

Arrival

Thrills and surprises!

TRAVEL PAGE

Andres Martin writes about his recent trip to Florida.

For years I have dreamed of visiting Florida, home of Disney World and fringed with warm sandy beaches and palm trees. When a long lost relative invited us out to stay, I jumped at this opportunity of a lifetime!

We flew out on an airbus. Our cousin met us at Orlando Airport and took us to his comfortable modern villa, which was to be home for our seven-night stay.

We spent our first three days at Universal Studios where 'the movies come to life'. We boarded a tram car which took us on an amazing ride with shocks and surprises at every turn. At one point, a model of 'Jaws' leapt out of the water and snapped at us, making everyone scream in terror. A few minutes later we were trapped in our tram car while King Kong snarled at us through the bars. There were quieter rides, too: We met The Lion King and took to the air aboard Dumbo the flying elephant.

We spent day four at Sea World. In this marvellous theme park, underwater glass tunnels allowed us to get really close to rare sea mammals, like the friendly-faced manatees. At Wild Arctic we became research scientists and took a simulated helicopter ride to an Arctic base. Here we learnt about polar bears, walruses, whales and seals, all in their natural environment.

Florida is the home of the alligator and I knew my trip would not be complete until I saw one. On day five we took a special tour to Babock Wilderness Adventures where we could get really get close to them in the wild. Our driver took us in an open vehicle through grassland and deep into the swamps where they were lurking. We even got to stroke a baby one - taking great care of our fingers as its teeth were razor-sharp!

We spent the last few days of our trip relaxing in the sunshine on some wonderful beaches. We collected rare shells and paddled round the bay, spotting birds and tree frogs around the mangroves.

We had a marvellous trip and came home with very heavy hearts. It really was the holiday of a lifetime!

4 Now answer the following questions.

1 The report comes from a page in a class newspaper. Does the writer think his readers (in this case, his fellow students) will be interested in:
   a) lots of details about his domestic arrangements?
   b) a list of facts?
   c) a colourful description of his main itinerary?

2 Do you think the writer makes the holiday sound attractive? Give reasons.

3 Why do you think the writer has divided the text into sections, rather than writing one long text?

4 Which tense does the writer use most? Could he use the Present Perfect (have seen/have visited, ...)for most of this report? Why?/Why not?

Planning

1 Complete this plan of Andres' report.

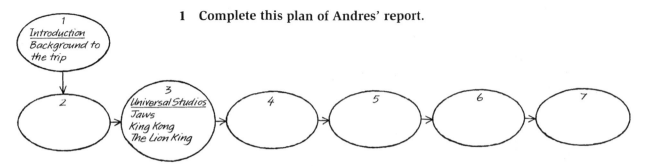

2 Now write a similar plan for your last holiday, real or imaginary!

Vocabulary jumble – Holidays

1 Sort these words into the correct columns.

sightseeing, bustling, leisure centre, exploring, museums, stunning, ruins, sunbathing, scary, tranquil, sports complex, picturesque, sights, art galleries, relaxing, exciting, castles, theme parks, marvellous.

Things to visit on holiday	Adjectives	Holiday activities
leisure centre	bustling	sightseeing
....	....	....
....	....	....
....	....	....

2 Can you add more words to each list?

Linking sentences 1

> **London** is famous for its history and traditions. It is also rich in culture.
>
> *Famous for its history and traditions, London is also rich in culture.*

Link the sentences below, beginning each new sentence with a past participle or an adjective as in the example above.

1 The Alhambra was built by the Moors during their occupation of Spain. It is a haven of coolness and tranquillity.
2 The beach is sheltered between high cliffs. It is a popular place for families.
3 The hotel is famous for its stunning views over the mountains. It is warm and welcoming.
4 The local people are shy with strangers. They lead a fascinating and totally different lifestyle to the tourists.

Linking sentences 2

1 Notice how we can join these sentences.

> I was talking to a friend. I suddenly saw the snake.
>
> *Talking to a friend, I suddenly saw the snake.*

When you link sentences in this way, check that the subject of each sentence is the same, and that you place the phrase in the right position. Otherwise you may end up with a rather improbable statement like this:
I suddenly saw the snake talking to a friend!

2 Say what is wrong with these sentences and then reorder them so that they say what the writer probably intended!

1 We saw an elephant driving across Africa last year.
2 That picture was given to me by a friend painted in the nineteenth century.
3 Filming in America, an alligator attacked a cameraman.
4 He found the baby and the wolf wearing a white dress.

Punctuation – Colons

Use a colon to divide two sentences, when the second sentence summarises, explains or enlarges the first.

> *There were quieter rides, too: we saw The Lion King and took to the air with Dumbo.*

A colon also introduces a list.

> *We saw lots of animals: whales, seals, walruses and polar bears.*

There are *no* punctuation marks or capital letters in this text. Add them in, where appropriate.

Sightseeing in London

we decided to see london the lazy way and took a boat down the thames on the way we listened to a fantastic commentary which was available in english or in translation if we preferred we got off at the tower of london and saw such a lot of things the crown jewels the beefeaters who guard the tower and the famous ravens.

Eating Out

There were plenty of bars and restaurants in covent garden we were lucky enough to find a table outside the food was good and not as expensive as we had anticipated we enjoyed it all the more as we were surrounded by pavement entertainers of all descriptions fire-eaters acrobats singers and skate board champions

Discussion

Use the following prompts to interview a partner about a holiday, real or imaginary. Use some of the language below in your answers.

What/best holiday/you/have?
Where exactly/you/go? Why/decide/go/there?
Who/go/with? Where/stay? For how long?
What/it/like?
It/be/famous/place? What/you/see and do? places of interest?
Where/go/evening? Theatres/shows?
You/sad/come home? Why?/Why not?

Written tasks

1   You came back from a marvellous holiday recently and have been asked to write a report on it for a local English-speaking magazine aimed at young people. If enough people like the sound of the holiday, you might be asked to accompany a group next year, all expenses paid! Make a plan and then write a report, using headings for the different sections.

2   You have just come back from a school trip. Write a report so that the next group of students who go will know what to expect. Report on the journey, what you saw and did during the day and how you spent the evenings. Group your ideas into sections with headings, as in the model text.

USEFUL TIPS

PLANNING

Try writing down a few section headings and then brainstorm ideas (single words only if you like) under each of the headings.

LINKING SENTENCES

Join your sentences together where appropriate in the ways you learnt in this Unit.

STYLE/REGISTER

Before you start, think carefully about the sort of reader you are writing for. Then decide how formal your language should be.

DRAFTING

Remember that you will probably need to write at least two drafts of your text before you have a reasonably clear and correct copy. Get your friends to help you check your writing for errors, if you can.

UNIT 17 — Notes and messages

Imagine – At the last minute, a friend rings and invites you to the cinema. The film begins in 15 minutes and it is a five-minute walk to the cinema. You have to leave a note for your Mum, to say where you have gone. Which of the following is the most appropriate? Why?

a

Dear Mum,
Gone to cinema. Back about 10.30.
Dinner in fridge.
If Alex rings, please get his new number.
Hope interview went well!

Love, Maria.

b

Dear Mum,

I am writing to tell you that I have gone to the cinema. I will be back at approximately half past ten.
I have placed your dinner in the refrigerator.
Should Alex ring, would you be so good as to obtain his new telephone number?
I do so hope your interview was successful.

With very best wishes,
Maria

c

Dear Mum,
Just a note to tell you that I have gone to the cinema. I will be back at about half past ten. Your dinner is in the refrigerator. If Alex rings, please can you get his new number.
I hope the interview went well.

Love
Maria

Using short forms

1 Look again at note a. Which of these statements are true?

In informal notes and messages:
a) you must always use pronouns
b) you don't always put the preposition
c) you must never leave out any part of the verb
d) you can sometimes leave out definite articles (*a, the*)
e) you can't use abbreviations
f) you must always use very polite language

Important!
A note or a message must be quick and easy to read. Short forms and abbreviations are useful but make sure that the meaning is still clear to the reader.

2 Look at these notes and messages. Can you say what they mean? What would you say if you were actually speaking to the person?

Mary
Gone to shops.
Key under mat.

Window Cleaner

Call next door for money.

Milkman
3 pints today please.

John,
Susan phoned.
Train delayed.
Now arriving 10 p.m.

Closed for lunch.
Open again 2 pm.

'Business' messages

The language used in memos (or faxes) is often more polite and formal than that used in messages to friends.

Look at the memo below and compare it with the messages you saw earlier.

Memo

To: Mr Sanchez
From: Toni

Date: 1/4/9-
Time: 5 p.m.

Mrs Andropoulos rang. Her plane is delayed. She will call again a.s.a.p. with revised time of arrival.

Vocabulary

These abbreviations are often found in notes and messages. Say what they mean. Can you add any more to the list?

a.m./p.m.	Mon./Tues.
&	etc.
i.e.	e.g.
NB	PTO
a.s.a.p.	No.

Understanding notes

Read the note below. Then write it out in full form, as if you were actually speaking to Anna.

Back Mon. morning. = I'll be back on Monday morning.

Anna

Hope you had a good holiday. Gone to stay with Thomas and Nikki for the weekend. Back Mon. morning.

Have left food in fridge. No milk though – sorry!

David called. Will ring again Sun. Sounds fed up – girlfriend problems again, I expect!

Rent due this Sat. Have left cheque under clock in living room.

Please feed cat. Tin in fridge.

Have a good weekend!

Mona

Being brief

Shorten the sentences below to make readable notes.

	Full sentence	Note
1	*I have lost my front door key!*	*Have lost front door key!*
2	Your dinner is on a tray in the refrigerator.	
3	Please can you take the dog for a walk.	
4	The TV is out of order.	
5	Please do not touch it.	

Writing short notes

Write a note for someone in your class. You can suggest going out this evening, ask for a date with their friend, or make some other request. Deliver your note. Then, write an answer to the note you receive and send it back.

Writing longer notes

Look at these notes which a policewoman made after visiting the scene of a burglary. She now needs to write a full report in complete sentences. Can you write the report for her?

> Burglary took place 3a.m. Family on holiday in Portugal. Back tomorrow (20 July).
> Window broken at back of house. Fingerprints on doors to living room and main bedroom. TV and video missing. Safe in bedroom empty. Have taken list of missing items from neighbour.
> Description of possible suspects:

Written tasks

1 **Write messages for these situations.**

   a) You arrange to go to the cinema with a friend from work at 4 p.m. While he is out of the office, you feel ill and decide to go home. Write a note to explain and suggest another day and time.

   b) You have been invited next door to a birthday party. Leave a note for your family to say where you are and what time you will be back.

2 **Some friends are coming to stay in your house but you have an appointment and can not be there to welcome them. Leave a note telling them where to leave their things and where to find something to eat and drink. Leave some instructions on how to operate the TV and say what else they can do until you get home.**

USEFUL TIPS

SHORT FORMS

Remember that when we write notes we often leave out pronouns, verbs, articles and prepositions. Do not leave out too much, though, or the meaning will be unclear to your reader.

FORMAT

Make sure your note is easy to read. Divide long notes into sections, with each important point on a new line.

(You need to write in note form when you are planning your compositions. Make sure your notes are clear enough to understand when you come back to them later!)

Pearson Education
Edinburgh Gate, Harlow,
Essex CM20 2JE, England
and Associated Companies throughout the world.

www.longman.com

© Addison Wesley Longman Limited 1996

First published 1996
Sixth impression 2004

Set in Slimbach 10pt/11pt

Printed in Spain
By Mateu Cromo, S.A. Pinto (MADRID)

ISBN 0 582 27922 4

Illustrated by Chris Pavely and Kathy Baxendale

Author's acknowledgement
With thanks to Margaret and David for all their support.

Acknowledgements
We are grateful to Faber and Faber Ltd for permission to
reproduce an abridged extract from the short story
'Crossing Over' from *Cold Marble and Other Stories*
by Catherine Storr.

We are grateful to the following for permission to reproduce copyright
photographs:

ACE Photo Agency for pages 21, 22, 32 (top); © Addison Wesley
Longman/Trevor Clifford for pages 32 (middle), 35 (top & bottom right);
Britstock-IFA for page 13, 54; J. Allan Cash Photolibrary for pages 32 (bottom
right), 40, 43 (left), 72 (middle & bottom); Greg Evans International for pages
44 (top), 72 (top); The Ronald Grant Archive for page 68 (middle); Robert
Harding Picture Library/James Davis/Int'l Stock for page 9 (right),/Storm
Stanley for page 44 (bottom left),/Nigel Francis for page 44 (bottom middle);
Hare Street & Little Parndon Housing Office for page 32 (left); Cover of
'Society Page' by Ruth Jean Dale reproduced with the kind permission of
Harlequin Enterprises Limited. First Published in Great Britain by Harlequin
Mills & Boon Limited, UK in 1995 for page 56 (top left); The Image Bank/Bill
Varie for page 24,/Nancy Brown for page 43 (bottom left),/Infocus
International for page 44 (bottom right); Katz Pictures/Simon Townsley for
page 8; The Kobal Collection for page 68 (left); Life File for pages 35 (middle),
43 (bottom right), 64 (right), 65; Network/Barry Lewis for page 64 (middle);
'Sassinak' reproduced courtesy of Orbit Books. Illustrated by Mark Harrison
for page 56 (bottom right); Penguin Books Ltd for page 56 (bottom left);
Retna Pictures/Peter Smith for page 9 (middle),/R. Brown for page 43 (top
right); Rex Features for page 68 (right); Tony Stone Worldwide/Bill Carter for
page 9 (left); Science Photo Library/Biophoto Associates for page 52; Cover of
'The Waitress' published by Scholastic Ltd for page 56 (top right); Telegraph
Colour Library for pages 21, 26, 36, 43 (top middle), 64 (left); Zefa Picture
Library for pages 12, 35 (bottom left), 63.